SEXUAL UTOPIA IN POWER:

THE FEMINIST REVOLT AGAINST CIVILIZATION

by

F. ROGER DEVLIN

Ministry of Love
Hollywood
2020

Cover image:
Lucas Cranach the Elder,
Judith with the Head of Holofernes, ca. 1530

Cover design by
Kevin I. Slaughter

Published in the United States by
MINISTRY OF LOVE

Hardcover: 978-1-64264-154-7
Paperback: 978-1-64264-155-4
EBook: 978-1-935965-90-9

CONTENTS

Note to the Reader:
No women were harmed in the writing of this book.

PREFACE

This is a book about the decline of virtue in women. In more contemporary parlance, it deals with feminism and the sexual revolution: two related socio-political movements which are both expression and cause of that decline.

Many people have written in criticism of these social phenomena already, but I have found most of this literature unsatisfying. Sex is among the most difficult subjects to write about; the writer is too close to his subject matter; limbic impulses (the male protective instinct, notably) substitute themselves for careful observation and interfere with cold analysis.

Moreover, sex is pre-eminently the domain in which normative discourse—*thou shalt nots* and, occasionally, *thou shalts*—drown out description, explanation, and rational understanding. This is understandable: sex is essential to the race's continued existence, yet is also potentially destructive. Practicality dictates keeping young people on the narrow path that is best both for themselves and for society, so the older discourse on sex was pretty much limited to the inculcation of marriage backed by religious sanctions (religious awe being the only force strong enough to counter something as primal as the sex instinct).

But a formerly effective method of regulating sexual behavior is one thing, a rational understanding of sex is something else entirely; and today, a correct understanding is what we most need. Traditional normative discussion of sex and marriage presupposes a social order in which lifelong monogamy enjoys social and legal sanction; the rearing of the young was intended to reinforce this already-existing order. Once moral and legal sanction have been withdrawn and the monogamous order destroyed, the old advice can even be harmful to the young man or woman who follows it. Plainly put, the young man or woman who "waits for marriage" in the contemporary West is likely either to wait forever or to be divorced within a few years.

The case is similar to the hoary advice to put money aside for a rainy day. As long as one is living in a reasonably healthy

economy, the advice is good; but in a context of currency inflation, where the value of money is being eroded faster than it can
be saved, saving becomes counterproductive.

Like inflation, sexual "liberation" turns the marketplace morally upside-down by actively punishing the virtuous and rewarding the vicious. Young people are gradually figuring this
out for themselves through painful experience, and if traditionalists have nothing better to offer them than repetition of their
grandparents' advice suited to a vanished order, they will lose
whatever tatters of authority they yet retain.

In this book, I explain what really happens when sex is "liberated," and why it happens. I like to think of my argument as—
borrowing a phrase from John Crowe Ransom—an *unorthodox
defense of orthodoxy*. The old order was, indeed, better than what
we have today; but its defenses have failed. The barbarians are
no longer at the gates—they are ourselves. To go on defending
"traditional marriage" in the contemporary world is to shut the
barn door after the horse has bolted. In a word, we must stop
thinking like "conservatives" and figure out how to rebuild a
tolerable order upon the facts of primitive human nature alone.

The main focus in what follows, along with all that is most
likely to surprise and possibly provoke the reader, is the account
I give of female sexuality. For the record, I hold no brief for my
own sex, but our faults are already sufficiently well-known and
widely denounced by feminists as well as traditionalists (often in
eerily similar ways). Women do not come in for the same kind of
criticism because (1) they are more complicated and harder to
understand than men; (2) they are masters of dissimulation,
even when not consciously trying to be; and (3) men have an
instinct to protect them—even from criticism. If this book sometimes sounds one-sided, it is because it seeks to correct this im-
balance. I am not a misogynist, but a misanthrope with a special
focus on women.

Boys and girls both come into the world as savages, and the
continuance of civilized life depends upon teaching them to control their instincts before they reach adulthood. Neither sex
should be criticized for having natural instincts which require
control, but both should be liable to criticism for failing to do so.

What I say about women's sexual *instincts* is meant to apply to all women, or at least to all normal women; but my criticism of contemporary female *behavior* refers only to women emblematic of the current *Zeitgeist*, those who have "liberated" themselves from the normal duties incumbent upon their sex in any healthy society. The objection that "not all women are like that" is always valid, of course, but a bit like defending the Black Death on the grounds that it did not, after all, kill *everybody*.

Indeed, when I read Theodore Roosevelt or Victorian sentimentalists rhapsodizing about the heroic self-sacrifice of wives and mothers, I do not feel that there necessarily exists any substantive difference between my view of women and theirs — rather, I would explain our differences by the different historical data sets with which we are working. Human nature and feminine nature may be constant, but they can express themselves in radically different ways under different circumstances. We have exchanged a set of incentives that raised women's behavior above that of the average man in favor of one which has allowed women to plunge themselves to depths previously unimagined.

In short, the modern West must face up to its systematic failure to properly socialize its young, but its girls in particular. This will require many persons to abandon cherished illusions. Here are a few of the things I attempt to explain in the essays ahead:

1. There is no more sex available to men in general today than there was before the sexual revolution; i.e., men in general did not gain at the expense of women from the sexual revolution.

2. Sex today, whether on college campuses or in the larger society, is not a "free for all."

3. Men do not "prey upon" women.

4. Women are not naturally monogamous.

5. Women do not naturally look for "worthy" men to marry; i.e., there is no moral component to female sexuality.

6. Our current problems would not be solved if only men would "man up" and accept their traditional responsibilities.

INTRODUCTION:

THE FACTS OF LIFE

Many sciences derive large bodies of surprising results from a few simple principles: the geometry of Euclid from its handful of postulates and definitions, or economics from the law of supply and demand. In studying the behavior of the sexes as well, nearly everything can be traced back to a single root cause: the *difference in quantity of gamete production*. Gametes are the sex cells, eggs and sperm, which fuse during fertilization. In every sexually reproducing species, one sex produces more gametes than the other. The difference can be extremely large: among humans, twelve million sperm per hour in men *vs.* four hundred eggs over the course of a lifetime in women. Higher gamete production is, indeed, the biological definition of "male"; when biologists discover an exotic new species, they determine which sex is which by comparing their rate of gamete production.

There is a trade-off between the number and size of gametes: an organism can produce more gametes if each one is small and simple. Thus, sperm are not only more numerous, but much smaller and easier to produce than eggs. Eggs are among the largest human cells.

Sexual reproduction is a riskier process and consumes more energy than asexual reproduction. How it first arose, we do not know. But we do know why it stuck around once it appeared: sexual reproduction allows for the rapid spread of beneficial mutations through the breeding pool. Indeed, scarcely anything deserving the name of evolution occurs before sexual reproduction arises—merely occasional random mutations.

The first sexually reproducing organisms were probably hermaphrodites, equipped with the reproductive organs of both sexes. Thus, while A's male organs were fertilizing the female organs of B, A's female organs might also be getting fertilized by a third party C. Indeed, there still exist primitive creatures of this sort.

It is also possible that the first sexually reproducing organisms did not differ substantially in the quantity or size of gametes they produced. But slight differences in both size and quantity must have occurred, if only by chance at first. And once this process started, the differences will quickly have grown. This is because there are advantages to both the small-and-many (male) approach and the large-and-few (female) approach. Both emergent males and emergent females are led by evolutionary pressures to capitalize on the advantages of their own peculiar strategy, which makes the difference between them self-reinforcing. In other words, over evolutionary time, female gametes tend to become ever larger and scarcer, while the male gametes become ever smaller and more numerous to maximize the odds that one of them will successfully find and mate with the increasingly scarce eggs. Hence, the overwhelming differences in gamete size and quantity found in humans.

Because of the scarcity of gametes which defines them, women are the limiting factor in human reproduction. A society of a thousand men and a single woman would be doomed, unable produce enough offspring from the one women to survive. But in a society composed of a thousand women and only one man, while the poor fellow might have his work cut out for him, he *could* eventually father children by all the women. In other words, while both sexes are essential to the process of reproduction, an individual man is of far lower value than an individual woman. In the language of economics, women have greater *marginal value* (for reproductive purposes) than men. This is why men are expected to protect women, up to and including the sacrifice of their lives; this is why women rather than men filled the Titanic's lifeboats. In Warren Farrell's words, men are the expendable sex.

It remains to be explained why more complex organisms such as ourselves are no longer hermaphrodites—why there are not merely two kinds of sex organs but two sexes, with each organism being of only one sex. This riddle appears to have been solved in the early 1990s by a computer engineer named Wirt Atmar, who experimented with computer modeling of biological processes. My account is derived from Steve Moxon's popularization of these ideas in *The Woman Racket*.[1]

The function of evolution is to perpetuate and spread reproductively valuable mutations, which are extremely rare, while getting rid of harmful ones, which are rather more common. Because most mutations are harmful, experimenting with them is a dangerous business. Nature does not squander reproductively valuable females on such a task; they must be kept safe and consecrated to the job of perpetuating the species. With males, on the other hand, nature can afford to experiment and lose a few (rather a lot, in fact).

The simplest way to isolate mutations from females would be for them to occur directly on the Y chromosome, but this is a rare occurrence because the Y chromosome is so small: it literally does not have enough room to contain genes for much more than male sex characteristics. Somewhat counterintuitively, mutations can also be isolated from females when they occur on the X chromosome. This is what happens in the case of sex-linked disorders which overwhelmingly affect men, including red-green color blindness, Hemophilia, and some forms of Muscular Dystrophy. Women inherit such mutations as easily as men, but their effects are almost always masked by the corresponding gene in the X chromosome they inherit from their mothers. This only works if the mutation involved is recessive.

Most mutations, of course, occur on one of the other twenty-three pairs of chromosomes. What happens in this case is that the mutations are more exposed to the process of natural selection in males than in females. Men far more than women test their own limits in ways bound to show up any weaknesses in their genetic makeup or clearly reveal any unusual strengths, e.g., in physical activity such as hunting and fighting. The effects of these differences are greatly multiplied by female sexual selection in favor of men with better genes. Even slight dif-

---

[1] Steve Moxon, *The Woman Racket: The New Science Explaining How the Sexes Relate at Work, at Play, and in Society* (Charlottesville, Va.: Imprint Academic, 2008).

ferences between genetic fitness in men can be perceived by women, who are naturally attuned to making such comparisons, and they translate into big differences in male reproductive success. This is especially true in a polygamous society, but the same effects occur in a more muted way under a system of monogamy, with males perceived as fit tending to marry earlier with (on average) more fertile females.

Most of what follows derives directly or indirectly from these simple facts.

SEXUAL UTOPIA IN POWER

It is well known that white birthrates worldwide have suffered a catastrophic decline in recent decades. During this same period, ours has become assuredly the most sex-obsessed society in the history of the world. Two such massive, concurrent trends are hardly likely to be unrelated. Many well-meaning conservatives agree in deploring the present situation, but do not agree in describing that situation or how it arose. Correct diagnosis is the first precondition for effective strategy.

The well-worn phrase "sexual revolution" ought, I believe, to be taken with more than customary seriousness. Like the French Revolution, the paradigmatic political revolution of modern times, it was an attempt to realize a utopia, but a sexual rather than political utopia. And like the French Revolution, it has gone through three phases: first, a libertarian or anarchic phase in which the utopia was supposed to occur spontaneously once old ways had been swept aside; second, a reign of terror, in which one faction seized power and attempted to realize its schemes dictatorially; and third, a "reaction" in which human nature gradually reasserted itself. We shall follow this order in the present essay.

TWO UTOPIAS

Let us consider what a sexual utopia is, and let us begin with men, who are in every respect simpler.

Nature has played a trick on men: production of spermatozoa occurs at a rate several orders of magnitude greater than female ovulation. This is a natural, not a moral, fact. Among the lower animals also, the male is grossly oversupplied with something for which the female has only a limited demand. This means that the female has far greater control over mating. The universal law of nature is that males display and females choose. Male peacocks spread their tails, females choose. Male rams butt horns, females choose. Among humans, boys try to impress girls—and the girls choose. Nature dictates that in the mating dance, the male must wait to be chosen.

A man's sexual utopia is, accordingly, a world in which no such limit to female demand for him exists. It is not necessary to resort to pornography for examples. Consider only popular movies aimed at a male audience, such as the James Bond series. Women simply cannot resist James Bond. He does not have to propose marriage, or even request dates. He simply walks into the room and they swoon. The entertainment industry turns out endless unrealistic images such as this. Why, the male viewer eventually may ask, cannot life actually be so? To some, it is tempting to put the blame on the institution of marriage.

Marriage, after all, seems to restrict sex rather drastically. Certain men figure that if sex were permitted both inside and outside of marriage there would be twice as much of it as formerly. They imagined there existed a large, untapped reservoir of female desire hitherto repressed by monogamy. To release it, they sought, during the early postwar period, to replace the seventh commandment with an endorsement of all sexual activity between "consenting adults." Every man could have a harem. Sexual behavior in general, and not merely family life, was henceforward to be regarded as a private matter. Traditionalists who disagreed were said to want to "put a policeman in every bedroom." This was the age of the Kinsey Report and the first appearance of *Playboy* magazine. Idle male daydreams had become a social movement.

This characteristically male sexual utopianism was a forerunner of the sexual revolution but not the revolution itself. Men are incapable of bringing about fundamental changes in heterosexual relations without the cooperation—the famed "consent"—of women. But the original male would-be revolutionaries did not understand the nature of the female sex instinct. That is why things have not gone according to their plan.

What is the special character of feminine sexual desire that distinguishes it from that of men?

It is sometimes said that men are polygamous and women monogamous. Such a belief is often implicit in the writings of male conservatives: women only want good husbands, but heartless men use and abandon them. Some evidence does appear, *prima facie*, to support such a view. One 1994 survey found that "while men projected they would ideally like 6 sex partners over the next year, and 8 over the next two years, women responded that their ideal would be to have only one partner over the next year. And over two years? The answer, for women, was still one."[1] Is not this evidence that women are naturally monogamous?

No it is not. Women know their own sexual urges are unruly, but traditionally have had enough sense to keep quiet about it. A husband's belief that his wife is naturally monogamous makes for his own peace of mind. It is not to a wife's advantage, either, that her husband understand her too well: knowledge is power. In short, we have here a kind of Platonic "noble lie" — a belief which is salutary, although false.

It would be more accurate to say that the female sexual instinct is *hypergamous*. Men may have a tendency to seek sexual variety, but women have simple tastes in the manner of Oscar Wilde: they are always satisfied with the best. By definition, only one man can be the best. These different male and female "sexual orientations" are clearly seen among the lower primates, e.g., in a baboon pack. Females compete to mate at the top, males to get to the top.

Women, in fact, have a distinctive sexual utopia corresponding to their hypergamous instincts. In its purely utopian form, it has two parts: (1) she mates with her incubus, the imaginary perfect man, and (2) he "commits," or ceases mating with all other women. This is the formula of much pulp romance fiction. The fantasy is strictly utopian, partly because no perfect man exists, but partly also because even if he did, it is logically impossible for him to be the exclusive mate of all the women who desire him.

It is possible, however, to enable women to mate hypergamously, i.e., with the most sexually attractive (handsome or socially dominant) men. In Aristophanes' *Ecclesiazusae*, the women of Athens stage a *coup d'état*. They occupy the legislative assembly

---

[1] Wendy Shalit, *A Return to Modesty* (New York: The Free Press), 1997, 90–91.

and barricade their husbands out. Then they proceed to enact a law by which the most attractive males of the city will be compelled to mate with each female in turn, beginning with the least attractive. That is the female sexual utopia in power. Aristophanes had a better understanding of the female mind than the average husband.

Hypergamy is not monogamy in the human sense. Although there may be only one "alpha male" at the top of the pack at any given time, which one it is changes over time. In human terms, this means the female is fickle, infatuated with no more than one man at any given time, but not naturally loyal to a husband over the course of a lifetime. In bygone days, it was permitted to point out natural female inconstancy. Consult, for example, Ring Lardner's humorous story "I Can't Breathe"—the private journal of an eighteen-year-old girl who wants to marry a different young man every week.[2] If surveyed on her preferred number of "sex partners," she would presumably respond one; this does not mean she has any idea who he is.

An important aspect of hypergamy is that it implies the rejection of most males. Women are not so much naturally modest as naturally vain. They are inclined to believe that only the "best" (most sexually attractive) man is worthy of them. This is another common theme of popular romance (the beautiful princess, surrounded by panting suitors, pined away hopelessly for a "real" man—until, one day . . . etc.).

This cannot be objectively true, of course. An average man would seem to be good enough for the average woman by definition. If women were to mate with all the men "worthy" of them they would have little time for anything else. To repeat, hypergamy is distinct from monogamy. It is an irrational instinct, and the female sexual utopia is a consequence of that instinct.

The sexual revolution in America was an attempt by women to realize their own utopia, not that of men. Female utopians came forward publicly with plans a few years after Kinsey and

---

[2] In *Selected Stories* (New York: Penguin Books, 1997), and many other collections.

Playboy. Helen Gurley Brown's *Sex and the Single Girl* appeared in 1962, and she took over *Cosmopolitan* magazine three years later. Notoriously hostile to motherhood, she explicitly encouraged women to use men (including married men) for pleasure.

ONE REVOLUTION

The actual outbreak of the sexual revolution occurred when significant numbers of young women began acting on the new utopian plan. This seems to have occurred on many college campuses in the nineteen-sixties. Women who took birth-control pills and committed fornication with any man who caught their fancy claimed they were liberating themselves from the slavery of marriage. The men, urged by their youthful hormones, frequently went along with this, but were not as happy about it as they are sometimes represented. Columnist Paul Craig Roberts recalls:

> I was a young professor when it all started and watched a campus turn into a brothel. The male students were perplexed, even the left-wing ones who had been taught to regard female chastity as oppression. I still remember the resident Marxist who, high on peyote, came to me to complain that "nice girls are ruining themselves."[3]

This should not be surprising. Most men prefer a virgin bride; this is a genuine aspect of male erotic desire favoring monogamy, and hence in constant tension with the impulse to seek sexual variety.

The young women, although hardly philosophers, did set forth arguments to justify their behavior. Most were a variation on the theme that traditional morality involved an unwarranted double standard. It was said that women who had promiscuous sex had been condemned as "sluts" while men who did the same were admired as "studs." It was pointed out that some men sought sex outside marriage and subsequently insisted on

---

[3] Paul Craig Roberts, "Losing the Ties That Bind," July 9, 2002, http://www.vdare.com/roberts/marriage.htm.

their brides being virgins. The common expression "fallen woman," and the absence of a corresponding expression "fallen man," was cited as further evidence of an unfair double-standard. The inference the women drew was that they, too, should thenceforward seek sex outside of marriage. This, of course, does not logically follow. They might have determined instead to set wayward men a good example by practicing monogamy regardless of men's own actions.

But let us ignore that for the moment and consider the premise of their argument concerning the double standard. Like most influential falsehoods, it involves a distortion, rather than a mere negation, of an important truth. It is plausible, and hence dangerous, because it resembles that truth.

The fundamental fallacy in the feminist critique of the double standard is the concealed premise that a man seducing a woman and a woman seducing a man are *doing the same thing.* They are not. It is a simple matter for nearly any young woman to find willing men, while most men cannot find large numbers of women willing to fornicate with them. A man who succeeds in seducing a lot of women is, therefore, beating the odds which nature has stacked against his sex. There is a sense in which some men may "admire" men who are unusually successful with women, but this implies no approval of fornication. No society has ever approved of men engaging in casual sex with women, and for obvious reasons: such behavior results in abandoned women and fatherless children who are a financial burden on innocent third parties. Accordingly, promiscuous men have traditionally been regarded as dissolute, dangerous, and dishonorable. They have been called by names such as "libertine" or "rake." The traditional rule of sexual conduct has been chastity outside of marriage, faithfulness within—for both sexes.

But it is true that a sexual indiscretion, whether fornication or adultery, has usually been regarded as a more serious matter in a woman than in a man, and socially sanctions for it have often been greater. In other words, while both sexes were supposed to practice monogamy, it was considered especially important for women to do so. Why is this?

In the first place, they tend to be better at it. This is not due to any moral superiority of the female, as many men are pleased to believe, but to their lower levels of testosterone and their slower sexual cycle: ovulation at the rate of one gamete per month.

Secondly, if women are all monogamous, the men will perforce be monogamous anyway: it is arithmetically impossible for polygamy to be the norm for men throughout a society because of the human sex ratio at birth.

Thirdly, the private nature of the sexual act and the nine month human gestation period mean that, while there is not normally doubt as to whom the mother of a particular baby is, there may well be doubt regarding the father. Female fidelity is necessary to assure the husband that his wife's children are also his.

Fourthly, women are, next to children, the main beneficiaries of marriage. Most men work their lives away at jobs they do not much care for in order to support wife and family. For women, marriage coincides with economic rationality; for a man, going to a prostitute is a better deal. Accordingly, chastity before marriage and fidelity within it are the very least a woman owes her husband. Indeed, on the traditional view, she owes him a great deal more. She is to make a home for him, return gratitude and loyalty for his support of her, and accept his position as head of the family.

Traditional concern for fallen women does not imply there are no "fallen men." Fornication is usually a sin of weakness, and undoubtedly many men who fall into it feel ashamed. The real double standard here is that few bother to sympathize with those men. Both men and women are more inclined to pity women. Some of the greatest male novelists of the nineteenth century devoted their best labors to the sympathetic portrayal of adulteresses. Men, by contrast, are expected to take full responsibility for their actions, no questions asked. In other words, this double standard favors women. So do most traditional sex roles, such as exclusively male liability to military service. The female responsibility to be the primary enforcer of monogamy is something of an exception.

What, after all, is the alternative to the double standard? Is it

practical to give sexually desperate young men exclusive responsibility to ensure no act of fornication ever takes place? Or
should women be locked up to make it impossible? Logically, a
woman must either have no mate, one mate, or more than one
mate. The first two choices are socially accepted; the third is not.
Such disapproval involves no coercion, however. Women who
insist on mating with multiple men *may* do so. But they are responsible for that behavior and its consequences, including enduring the social disapproval—mainly from other women—
which such behavior entails.

The fact is that women generally do not show any interest in
mating with multiple men in the absence of financial incentives.
So their complaints about the so-called double standard are not
perfectly sincere. Why, then, do so many women raise the issue?

I believe it is because women are attracted to men *whom other
women find attractive*. These, of course, are the men that have
been most successful with other women—in other words, the
"studs." The admiration women claim "studs" receive is in reality female lust.

Women do not complain about the double standard because
they are interested in having multiple mates, but because they
would like to have access to men *who have had multiple mates*—
without facing social disapproval. And they have no more
"right" to live out such fantasies than men do theirs.

Women's complaints about double standards refer only to
the few which seem to favor men. They unhesitatingly take advantage of those which favor themselves. Wives in modern,
two-income marriages, for example, typically assume that
"what I earn is mine; what he earns is ours." Young women insist on their "independence," but assume they are entitled to
male protection should things get sticky.

But the ultimate expression of modern female hypocrisy is
the assertion of a right to adultery for women only. This view is
clearly implied in much contemporary self-help literature aimed
at women. Titles like *Get Rid of Him* and *Ditch That Jerk* are
found side-by-side *Men Who Can't Love: How to Spot a Commitmentphobic Man*. In short, I demand loyalty from you, but you
have no right to expect it of me. Many women seem sincerely

unable to sense a contradiction here. Perhaps, as Schopenhauer thought, the female is not naturally provided with a sense of justice. Justice is, after all, a virtue of leaders; it is of little use in nurturing children.

However that may be, the modern woman clearly wants the benefits of a traditional marriage but is unwilling to pay the costs; she wants a man to marry her without her having to marry the man. It is the eternal dream of irresponsible freedom: in the feminist formulation, freedom for women, responsibility for men.

Men, by contrast, usually accept that their demand for faithfulness from their wives entails a reciprocal duty of faithfulness *to* their wives. In fact, I am inclined to believe most men lay too much stress on this. For a man, fidelity in marriage should be a matter of preserving his own honor and ensuring that he is able to be a proper father to all his children; his wife's feelings are a secondary matter, as are his own. In any case, the marriage vow is carefully formulated to enunciate a reciprocity of obligations; both the man and woman pledge faithfulness for life. Given innate sex differences, it is not possible to eliminate the double-standard any more than marriage already has.

FALLOUT OF THE REVOLUTION: "DATE RAPE"

A few years into the sexual revolution, shocking reports began to appear of vast numbers of young women—from one quarter to half—being victims of rape. Shock turned to bewilderment when the victims were brought forward to tell their stories. The "rapists," it turns out, were never lying in wait for them in remote corners, were not armed, did not attack them. Instead, these "date rapes" occur in private places, usually college dormitory rooms, and involve no threats or violence. In fact, they little resemble what most of us think of as rape.

What was going on here?

Take a girl too young to understand what erotic desire is and subject her to several years of propaganda the effect that she has a right to have things any way she wants them in this domain—with no corresponding duties to God, her parents, or anyone else. Do not give her any guidance as to what it might be good for her to want, how she might try to regulate her own conduct, or what qualities she ought to look for in a young man. Teach her, furthermore, that the notion of natural differences between the sexes is a laughable superstition that our enlightened age is gradually overcoming—with the implication that men's sexual desires are no different from or more intense than her own. Meanwhile, as she matures physically, keep her protected in her parents' house, sheltered from responsibility.

Then, at age seventeen or eighteen, take her suddenly away from her family and all the people she has ever known. She can stay up as late as she wants! She can decide for herself when and how much to study! She's making new friends all the time, young women and men both. It's no big deal having them over or going to their rooms; everybody is perfectly casual about it. What difference does it make if it's a boy she met at a party? He seems like a nice fellow, like others she meets in class.

Now let us consider the young man she is alone with. He is neither a saint nor a criminal, but, like all normal young men of college years, he is intensely interested in sex. There are times he cannot study without getting distracted by the thought of some young woman's body. He has little experience with girls, and most of it unhappy. He has been rejected a few times without much ceremony, and it was more humiliating than he cares to admit. He has the impression that for other young men things are not as difficult: "everybody knows," after all, that since the 1960s men get all the sex they like, right? He is bombarded with talk about sex on television, in the words to popular songs, in rumors about friends who supposedly "scored" with this or that girl. He begins to wonder if there isn't something wrong with him.

Furthermore, he has received the same education about sex as the girl he is now with. He has learned that people have the right to do anything they want. The only exception is rape. But that is hardly even relevant to him; he is obviously incapable of doing something like that.

He has also been taught that there are no important differences between the sexes. This means, of course, that girls want sex just as badly as he does, though they slyly pretend otherwise. And are not their real desires verified by all those *Cosmopolitan* magazine covers he sees constantly at the grocery store? If women are so eager to read such stuff, why should it be so damned difficult to find just one girl willing to go to bed with him?

But tonight, finally, something seemed to click. He met a girl at a party. They chatted, perhaps drank a bit: all smiles, quite unlike the girls who had been so quick about rejecting him in High School. She even let him come to her room afterwards (or came to his). It doesn't take a genius to figure out what she is thinking, he says to himself. This is a tremendously important moment for him; every ounce of his self-respect is at stake. He is confused, and his heart is pounding, but he tries to act as if he knows what he is doing. She seems confused, too, and he meets no more than token resistance (or so it seems to him). He doesn't actually enjoy it and isn't sure whether she does either. But that is beside the point; it only matters that he can finally consider himself a man. Later on they can talk about what terms they want to be on, whether she will be his regular girlfriend, etc. Matrimony is not exactly uppermost in his mind, but he might not rule it out—eventually. He asks her how she feels afterwards, and she mumbles that she is "okay." This sets his mind at rest. An awkward parting follows.

Later that night or the next morning our young woman is trying to figure out what in hell has happened to her. Why had he gotten so pushy all of a sudden? Didn't he even want to get to know her first? It was confusing; it all happened so quickly. Sex, she had always heard, was supposed to be something wonderful; but this she had not enjoyed at all. She felt somehow used.

Of course, at no point does it enter her mind to question her own right to have been intimate with the young man if she had wanted to. Moral rule number one, we all know, is that all sex between consenting adults is licit. She just isn't sure whether she had really wanted this. In fact, the more she thinks about it, the more certain she feels that she hadn't. But if she hadn't wanted it, then it was against her will, wasn't it? And if it was against her will, that means . . . she's been raped?

I sympathize with the young woman, in view of a miseducation which might have been consciously designed to leave her unprepared for the situation she got herself into. But as to the question of whether she was raped, the answer must be a clear *no.*

Let me explain by means of an analogy with something less emotionally laden. Consider someone who purchases a lottery ticket which does not win the prize. Suppose he were to argue as follows: "I put my money down because I wanted the prize. I wouldn't have paid if I had known I was going to lose; therefore I have been deprived of my money against my will; therefore I am the victim of theft." No one would accept this argument as valid. Why shouldn't we?

For the very good reason that it denies the fundamental principle behind all personal responsibility. Those who want to make their own choices in life must be willing to accept the consequences of those choices. Consider the alternative: if every loser in a lottery were entitled to a refund there would be no money left for the prize, and so no lottery. For similar reasons, most civilized institutions depend upon people taking responsibility for their actions, keeping agreements, and fulfilling obligations regardless of whether or not they happen to like the consequences.

The grandmother of the young woman in our story was unaware that she possessed a "right" to sleep with any boy who took her fancy—nor to invite him to her bedroom and expect nothing to happen. It was the male and female sexual utopians of the postwar period who said women should be allowed unlimited freedom to choose for themselves in such matters. Unfortunately, they did not lay much stress on the need to accept the consequences of poor choices. Instead, they treated the moral and social norms women in particular had traditionally used to guide themselves as wholly irrational barriers to pleasure. Under their influence, two generations of women have been led to believe that doing as they please should lead to happiness and involve no risk. Hence the moral sophistry of "I didn't like it; *ergo* I didn't want it; *ergo* it was against my will."

To anyone who believes that a society of free and responsible persons is preferable to one based on centralized control, the reasoning of the date-rape movement is ominous. The demand that law rather than moral principle and common prudence should protect women in situations such as I have described could only be met by literally "putting a policeman in every bedroom." However much we may sympathize with the misled young people involved (and I mean the men as well as the women), we must insist that it is no part of our responsibility to create an absolutely safe environment for them, nor to shield them from the consequences of their own behavior, nor to insure that sex will be their path to happiness. Because there are some things of greater importance than the pain they have suffered, and among these are the principle of responsibility upon which the freedom of all of us depends.

It was never the traditional view that a woman's erotic power over men was anything she possessed unconditional personal rights over. Instead, the use to which she put this natural power was understood to be freighted with extensive responsibilities — to God, her family, the man to whom she gave herself, the children produced by the union, and her own *long term* well-being. In order to fulfill her obligations as creature, daughter, wife, and mother she required considerable powers of self-control. This cultivated and socially reinforced sexual self-control was known as modesty. It required chiefly the duty of chastity before marriage and fidelity within marriage; secondarily, it involved maintaining a certain demeanor toward men — polite but reserved.

Now, every duty does imply a right: if we have a duty to provide for our children or defend our country we necessarily possess the right to do so as well. Formerly, insofar as sexual rights were recognized, they were understood to have this character of resting upon duties. Thus, a woman did indeed have the right to refuse the sexual advances of any man not her husband. But this was only because she was not understood to have any moral right to *accept* a proposal of fornication or adultery (even in the absence of legal sanctions therefore).

The reason rape was regarded as a particularly odious form of assault is that it violated this superpersonal moral principle by which a woman subordinated her momentary private desires to the well-being of those closest to her. Modesty had to be respected, or else protected, if it was to perform its essential social function of guarding the integrity of families.

Under Roman law it was not considered a serious crime to rape a prostitute: a man could not violate the modesty of a woman who had none to violate. In later European law it was made criminal to rape even prostitutes. But this does not mean that the concept of rape had been divorced from that of feminine modesty; it was rather that law came to recognize and protect the possibility of repentance for immodesty. (Christianity is relevant here.)

The sexual revolution asserted the right of each individual to sex on his or her own terms—in other words, a right of perfect selfishness in erotic matters. One effect of this change was to eliminate the moral dignity of feminine modesty. It was not to be forbidden, of course, but was henceforward to be understood as no more than a personal taste, like anchovies or homosexuality. When the initial excitement of abandoned restraint had died down it was noticed that the promised felicity had not arrived. And one reason, it was soon realized, was that the terms men wished to set for sexual conduct were not identical to those desired by women. This being so, the granting to men of a right to sex on their own terms necessarily involved the denial of such a right to women. The anarchy with which the sexual revolution began was, therefore, necessarily a passing phase.

FROM SEXUAL ANARCHY TO SEXUAL TERROR

It is a cliché of political philosophy that the less self-restraint citizens are able to exercise, the more they must be constrained from without. The practical necessity of such a trade-off can be seen in such extraordinary upheavals as the French and Russian Revolutions. First, old and habitual patterns and norms are thrown aside in the name of freedom. When the ensuing chaos becomes intolerable, some group with the requisite ambition, self-assurance, and ruthlessness succeeds in forcibly imposing its own order on the weakened society. This is what gradually happened in the case of the sexual revolution also, with the role of Jacobins/Bolsheviks being assumed by the feminists.

Human beings cannot do without some social norms to guide them in their personal relations. Young women cannot be expected to work out a personal system of sexual ethics in the manner of Descartes reconstructing the universe in his own mind. If you cease to prepare them for marriage, they will seek guidance wherever they can find it. In the past thirty years they have found it in feminism, simply because the feminists have out-shouted everyone else.

After helping to encourage sexual experimentation by young women, feminism found itself able to capitalize on the unhappiness which resulted. Their program for rewriting the rules of human sexual behavior is in one way a continuation of the liberationists' utopian program and in another way a reaction against it. The feminists approve the notion of a right to do as one pleases without responsibilities toward others; they merely insist that only women have this right.

Looking about them for some legal and moral basis for enforcing this novel claim, they hit upon the age-old prohibition against rape. Feminists understand rape, however, not as a violation of a woman's chastity or marital fidelity, but of her merely personal wishes. They are making use of the ancient law against rape to enforce not respect for feminine modesty but obedience to female whims. Their ideal is not the man whose self-control permits a woman to exercise her own, but the man who is subservient to a woman's good pleasure—the man who behaves, not like a gentleman, but like a dildo.

But mere disregard of a woman's personal wishes is manifestly not the reason men have been disgraced, imprisoned, in some societies even put to death for the crime of rape. On the new view, in which consent rather than the marriage bond is the issue, the same sexual act may be a crime on Monday or Wednesday and a right on Tuesday or Thursday according to the shifts in a woman's mood. Feminists claim rape is not taken seriously enough; perhaps it would be better to ask how it could be taken seriously at all once we begin defining it as they do. If women want to be free to do as they please with men, after all, why should not men be free to do as they please with women?

Indeed, the date rape campaign owes its success only to the lingering effect of older views. Feminists themselves are not confused about this; they write openly of "redefining rape." Of course, for those of us who still speak traditional English, this amounts to an admission that they are falsely accusing men.

One might have more sympathy for the "date rape victims" if they wanted the men to marry them, feared they were ruined for other suitors, and were prepared to assume their own obligations as wives and mothers. But this is simply not the case. The date rape campaigners, if not the confused young women themselves, are hostile to the very idea of matrimony, and never propose it as a solution. They want to jail men, not make responsible husbands of them. This is far worse than shotgun marriage, which at least allowed the man to act as father to the child he had sired.

And what benefit do women derive from imprisoning men as date rapists apart from gratification of a desire for revenge? Seeing men punished may even confirm morally confused women in their mistaken sense of victimhood—resentment tends to feed upon itself, like an itch that worsens with scratching. Women are reinforced in the belief that it is their right for men's behavior to be anything they would like it to be. They become less inclined to treat men with respect or to try to learn to understand or compromise with them. In a word, they learn to think and behave like spoiled children, expecting everything and willing to give nothing.

Men, meanwhile, respond to this in ways that are not difficult to predict. They may not (at first) decline sexual liaisons with such women, because the woman's moral shortcomings do not have too great an effect upon the sexual act itself. But, quite rationally, they will avoid any deeper involvement with them. So women experience fewer, shorter and worse marriages and "relationships" with men. But they do not blame themselves for the predicament they are in; they refuse to see any connection between their own behavior and their loneliness and frustration. Thus we get ever more frequent characterizations of men as rapists and predators who mysteriously refuse to commit.

Indeed, the only people profiting from the imposition of the new standards are the feminists who invented them. The survival of their movement depends on a continuing supply of resentful women who believe their rights are being violated; one can only admit that the principles which undergird the date rape campaign are admirably designed to guarantee such a supply. Feminism is a movement that thrives on its own failures; hence, it is very difficult to reverse.

Merriam-Webster's Collegiate Dictionary, 11th edition, lists the first recorded use of the term 'date rape' as 1975. Within a few years we find Thomas Fleming of *Chronicles*, for example, employing the expression as uncritically as any feminist zealot.[4] A second instrument of the feminist reign of sexual terror, "sexual harassment," similarly made its first appearance in 1975. In less than a generation it has become a national industry providing a comfortable living for many people. Yet again we find this revolutionary concept blithely accepted by many male traditionalists. They are content to accept without argument that there exists a widespread problem of men "harassing" women and that "something must be done about it." My first thought would be: What did the Romans do about it? What did the Christian Church do about it? How about the Chinese or the Aztecs? The obvious answer is that none of them did anything about it, because the concept has only recently developed within the context of the feminist movement. Is this not cause for suspicion? Why are men so quick to adopt the language of their declared enemies?

The thinking behind the sexual harassment movement is that women are entitled to "an environment free from unwanted sexual advances." What sort of advances are unwanted? In plain English, those made by unattractive men. Anyone who has been forced to endure a corporate anti-harassment video can see that what is being condemned is merely traditional male courtship behavior.

The introduction of harassment law was accompanied by a campaign to inform young women of the new entitlement. Col-

---

[4] "Beware of What You Pray For," February 11, 2005, and elsewhere.

leges, for example, instituted harassment committees one of whose stated purposes was "to encourage victims to come forward." (I saw this happening up close.) The agitators *wanted* as many young women as possible accusing unsuccessful suitors of wrongdoing. And they had considerable success; many women unhesitatingly availed themselves of the new dispensation. Young men found they risked visits from the police for flirting or inviting women on dates.

This female bullying should be contrasted with traditional male chivalry. Men, at least within Western Civilization, have been socialized into extreme reluctance to use force against women. This is not an absolute principle: few would deny that a man has a right of self-defense against a woman attempting to kill him. But many men will refuse to retaliate against a woman under almost any lesser threat. This attitude is far removed from the feminist principle of equality between the sexes. Indeed, it seems to imply a view of men as naturally dominant: it is a form of *noblesse oblige*. And it is not, so far as I can see, reducible to any long-term self-interest on the part of a man; in other words, it is a principle of honor. The code of chivalry holds that a man has no moral right to use force against women simply because he *can* do so.

An obvious difficulty with such a code is that it is vulnerable to abuse by its beneficiaries. I had a classmate in grade school who had heard it said somewhere that "boys are not supposed to hit girls." Unfortunately, she interpreted this to mean that it was acceptable for girls to hit boys, which she then proceeded to do. She became genuinely indignant when she found that they usually hit back.

The special character of *noblesse oblige* is that it does not involve a corresponding entitlement on the part of the beneficiary. On the traditional view, a man should indeed be reluctant to use force against women, but women have no right to presume upon this. The reluctance is elicited by a recognition of women's weakness, not commanded as a recognition of their rights.

Perhaps because women are the weaker sex, they have never developed any similar inhibitions about using force against men. In a traditionally ordered society, this does not present difficulties, because a woman's obligations to her husband are clearly understood and socially enforced. But the situation changes when millions of spoiled, impressionable young women have been convinced men are "harassing" them and that the proper response is to appeal to force of law and the police powers of the state. Men are being denied due process, ruined professionally, and threatened with particularly harsh punishments for any retaliation against the women accusing them of a newly-invented and deliberately ill-defined crime. They may, for prudential reasons, outwardly conform to the new rules. But it is unlikely that the traditional reluctance *in foro interno* to use force against women can long survive the present pattern of female behavior. Women would do well to ponder this.

RETURN OF THE PRIMITIVE

Public discussion of the sexual revolution has tended to focus on date rape and "hook-ups," that is, on what *is* taking place, rather than on the formation of stable families that is *not* taking place. This creates an impression that there really is "more sex" for men today than before some misguided girls misbehaved themselves forty years ago. People speak as if the male sexual utopia of a harem for every man has actually been realized.

It is child's play to show that this cannot be true. There is roughly the same number of male as female children (not quite: there are about 5% more live male births than female. There is not a girl for every boy.) What happens when female sexual desire is liberated is not an increase in the total amount of sex available to men, but a redistribution of the existing supply. Society becomes polygamous. A situation emerges in which most men are desperate for wives, but most women are just as desperately throwing themselves at a very few exceptionally attractive men. These men, who have always found it easy to get a mate, now get multiple mates.

A characteristic feature of decadent societies is the recrudescence of primitive, precivilized cultural forms. That is what is happening to us. Sexual liberation really means the Darwinian mating pattern of the baboon pack reappears among humans.

Once monogamy is abolished, no restriction is placed on a

woman's choices. Hence, all women choose the same few men. If Casanova had 132 lovers it is because 132 different women chose him. Such men acquire harems, not because they are predators, but because they happen to be attractive. The problem is not so much male immorality as simple arithmetic; it is obviously impossible for every woman to have *exclusive* possession of the most attractive man. If women want to mate simply as their natural drives impel them, they must, rationally speaking, be willing to share their mate with others.

But, of course, women's attitude about this situation is not especially rational. They expect their alpha-man to "commit." Woman's complaining about men's failure to commit, one suspects, means merely that they are unable to get a highly attractive man to commit *to them*; rather as if an ordinary man were to propose to Helen of Troy and complain of her refusal by saying "women don't want to get married."

Furthermore, many women are sexually attracted to promiscuous men because, not in spite, of their promiscuity. This can be explained with reference to the primate pack. The "alpha male" can be identified by his mating with many females. This is probably where the sluts-and-studs double standard argument came from—not from any social approval of male promiscuity, but from female fascination with it. Male "immorality" (in traditional language) can be attractive to females. Thus, once polygamous mating begins, it tends to be self-reinforcing.

Students of animal behavior have learned that the presence of a female decoy or two near a male makes real females more likely to mate with that particular male. Among human females also, nothing succeeds like success. I hear anecdotes about women refusing to date thirtyish bachelors because, "if he's never been married, there must be something wrong with him." In college I observed decent, clean-living men left alone while notorious adulterers had no difficulty going from one girlfriend to the next.

Commentators on contemporary mores rarely show awareness of this irrationality in female mate selection. I recall seeing an article some years ago in which a planned new college was touted as a boon to young women seeking "Christian husbands," on the naive assumption that they must be doing so. There was no talk of helping young men find faithful wives, of course.

MODERN CHIVALRY

Both men and women find it easier to sympathize with young women than with young men. In the case of male observers a kind of rescue fantasy is probably at work. The literature and folklore of the world is replete with stories of heroes rescuing innocent maidens from the clutches of villains: too much for it to be an accident. The damsel in distress scenario appeals to something deeply rooted in men's minds, and probably natural. Most likely it is merely a self-congratulatory interpretation of mate competition. Men project their unruly sexual instincts onto others, who are thus cast into the role of predators.

In the contemporary world, the male protective instinct often perversely expresses itself in support for feminist causes: for example, chiming in with the denunciation of harassers and date rapists. This is a form of gallantry singularly well-adapted to the sedentary habits of the modern male, involving neither risk nor sacrifice. Examples abound in the conservative press. College men are regularly spoken of as preying upon women—who are in fact quite old enough to be married and starting a family. Joseph Farah of *World Net Daily* commends a wife for murdering her unfaithful husband. There are calls for bringing back shotgun marriage and the death penalty for rapists. If only sufficiently draconian punishments can be meted out to villainous males, the reasoning seems to go, everything will be alright again. The fundamental error in such thinking is its failure to recognize that the female largely controls the mating process.

Shrewd women have long known how to manipulate the male protective urge for their own ends. The feminist attack on heterosexuality and the family is directed against husbands and fathers for reasons of public relations. No one will sign up for a campaign against women or children, but many men can easily be made to condemn other men. The result is that young men today are in an impossible situation. If they seek a mate they are predators; if they find one they are date rapists; if they want to avoid the whole ordeal they are immature and irresponsible for not committing. We have gone from a situation where it seemed everything was permitted to one where nothing is permitted. Marriage as a binding legal contract has been done away with, and young men are still supposed to believe it is wrong for them to seek sex outside of marriage. It is not prudent to put this much strain on human nature.

Meanwhile, the illusion of there being "too much sex" has lead to proposals for "abstinence education," provided by government schools and paid for with tax money. The geniuses of establishment conservatism may need a gentle reminder that the human race is not perpetuated through sexual abstinence. They might do better to ponder how many families have not formed and how many children have not been born due to overzealous attempts to protect young women from men who might have made good husbands and fathers.

THE REVOLUTION DESTROYS SEX

So far we have focused on female promiscuity, and undoubtedly it is a serious problem. But there are two ways for women not to be monogamous: by having more than one mate and . . . by having less than one. Let us now consider the spinsters as well as the sluts.

Here again I would warn against a misconception common among male writers: the assumption that young women *not* having sexual relations with men must be paragons of chastity. In fact, there are numerous reasons besides religious or moral principle which can keep a woman from taking a mate, and some of these now operate more strongly than before the sexual revolution. Consider the following passage from *A Return to Modesty* by Wendy Shalit:

> "Pfffffft!" sexual modesty says to the world, "I think *I'm* worth waiting for. . . . So not you, not you, not you, and not *you* either."
> This is certainly not modest. As one 27-year-old Orthodox woman put it to me . . . "the daughters of Israel

are not available for public use." She was taking obvious, almost haughty, satisfaction in the fact that she wasn't sleeping around with just *anyone*.[5]

This is pure illusion, a consequence of natural female hypergamy and not dependent on any actual merit in the woman. But it may be a socially useful illusion. If a woman believes she is "too good" to sleep around, this may help keep her faithful to her husband. Marriage, in other words, is a way of channeling female hypergamy in a socially useful way. (We frequently hear of the need to channel the male sexual instinct into marriage and family, but not the female; this is a mistake.)

In any case, hypergamy, as above noted, implies rejection maximization: if only the best is good enough, almost everyone is not good enough. Rather than cheapening herself, as observers tend to assume, modern woman may be pricing herself out of the market. It used to be commonly said that a woman who thinks she is too good for any man "may be right, but more often — is left." Why might this be an especial danger for women today?

Formerly, most people lived parochial lives in a world where even photography did not exist. Their notions of sexual attractiveness were limited by their experience. Back in my own family tree, for example, there was a family with three daughters who grew up on a farm adjoining three others. As each girl came of age, she married a boy from one of the neighboring farms. They did not expect much in a husband. It is probable all three went through life without ever seeing a man who looked like Cary Grant.

But by the 1930's millions of women were watching Cary Grant two hours a week and silently comparing their husbands with him. For several decades since then the entertainment industry has continued to grow and coarsen. Finally the point has been reached that many women are simply not interested in meeting any man who does not look like a movie star. While it is not possible to make all men look like movie stars, it is possi-

---

[5] Shalit, *A Return to Modesty*, pp. 131–32.

ble to encourage women to throw themselves at *or hold out for* the few who do, i.e., to become sluts or spinsters, respectively. Helen Gurley Brown raked in millions doing precisely this. The brevity of a woman's youthful bloom, combined with a mind not yet fully formed at that stage of life, always renders her vulnerable to unrealistic expectations. The sexual revolution is in part a large-scale commercial exploitation of this vulnerability.

Yes, men are also, to their own detriment, continually surrounded with images of exceptionally attractive women. But this has less practical import, because — to say it once more — *women choose.* Even plain young women are often able to obtain sexual favors from good-looking or socially dominant men; they have the option to be promiscuous. Many women do not understand that ordinary young men do not have that option.

Traditionalists sometimes speak as if monogamy were a cartel whose purpose was to restrict the amount of sex available to men artificially so as to drive up the price for the benefit of women. (That is roughly what the male sexual utopians believed also.) But this would require that men be able to raise their bid, i.e., make themselves more attractive at will. Monogamy does not get women as a group more desirable mates than would otherwise be available to them. In sex as in other matters the buyers, not the sellers, ultimately determine the price. And the buyers, by and large, are merely average men.

Furthermore, many young women appear to believe that any man who attempts to meet them *ipso facto* wishes to take them as a mate. Partly this is youthful naiveté; partly a result of the disintegration of socially agreed upon courtship procedures; and partly due to the feminist campaign to label male courtship behavior "harassment." So they angrily reject every advance they receive during their nubile years as if these were merely crude sexual propositioning. As they enter their late-twenties, it gradually dawns on them that it might be prudent to accept at least a few date-requests. They are then astonished to discover that the men usually take them out once or twice and stop calling. They claim the men are leading them on. They believe themselves entitled to a wedding ring in return for the great condescension of finally accepting a date. Just as some men think the world owes them a living, these women think the world owes them a husband.

When a man asks a woman out, he is only implying that he is willing to *consider* her as a mate: he might conceivably offer her a ring if she pleases him enough on further acquaintance. Most dates do not result in marriage proposals. There is no reason why they should. Rather than being blamed for not committing, such men should be commended for sexual self-control and the exercise of caution in mate-seeking. Many men have been only too happy to marry the first girl who is nice to them.

To summarize: the encouragement of rejection maximization and unrealistic expectations is one reason (unrelated to modesty) that many women today do not reproduce. A second is what I call parasitic dating, a kind of economic predation upon the male by the female. Let me explain.

The decline of matrimony is often attributed to men now being able to "get what they want" from women without marrying them. But what if a woman is able to get everything *she* wants from a man without marriage? Might she not also be less inclined to "commit" under such circumstances? In truth, a significant number of women seek primarily attention and material goods from men. They are happy to date men they have no romantic interest in merely as a form of entertainment and a source of free meals and gifts. A man can waste a great deal of money and time on such a woman before he realizes he is being used.

Family life involves sacrifice; a good mother *devotes herself* to her children. Parasitic daters are takers, not givers; they are not fit for marriage or motherhood. Their character is usually fixed by the time a man meets them. Since he cannot change them, the only rational course is to learn to identify and avoid them.

A third obstacle to female reproduction is date-rape hysteria. The reader may consult the first couple chapters of Katie Roiphe's *The Morning After*.[6] At an age when women have traditionally actively sought mates, they now participate in "take

[6] Katie Ropihe, *The Morning After: Sex, Fear and Feminism on Campus*, (Boston: Back Bay Books, 1994).

back the night" marches, "rape awareness" campaign and self-defense classes involving kicking male dummies in the groin. These young women seem less afraid of anything men are actually doing than they are of male sexual desire itself. In the trenchant words of columnist Angela Fiori "the campus date-rape campaigns of the early 1990s weren't motivated by a genuine concern for the well-being of women. They were part of an ongoing attempt to delegitimize heterosexuality to young, impressionable women by demonizing men as rapists."[7] Self-defense training, for example, really serves to inculcate a defensive *mentality* toward men, making trust and intimacy impossible.

Part of the transition to womanhood has always been learning to relate to men. Attempts to pander to girls' irrational fears are now keeping many of them in a state of arrested development. There is little that individual men can do about this, nor is there any reason they should be expected to. Who would want to court a girl encased in an impenetrable psychic armor of suspicion?

Once again, well-meaning male traditionalists have not been free of fault in their reactions to this situation. Fathers encourage self-defense classes and date-rape paranoia on the assumption that their daughters' safety overrides all other concerns. Eventually they may start wondering why they have no grandchildren.

Fourthly, many women are without a mate for the simple reason that they have abandoned their men. Women formally initiate divorce about two thirds of the time. Most observers agree, however, that this understates matters: in many cases where the husband formally initiates, it is because his wife wants out of the marriage. Exact data are elusive, but close observers tend to estimate that women are responsible for about nine-tenths of the divorcing and breaking-up: men do not love them and leave them, but love them and *get left by* them. Many young women, indeed, believe they want marriage when all

---

[7] Angela Fiori, "Feminism's Third Wave," May 23, 2003, http://www.lewrockwell.com/orig/fiori3.html.

they really want is a wedding (think of bridal magazines). The common pattern is that women are the first to want into marriage and the first to want out. Of course, it is easy enough to *get* married; the difficulty is living happily ever after.

Typically, the faithless wife does not intend to remain alone. But some men have scruples about involving themselves with divorcées; they wonder "whose wife is this I'm dating?" There are also merely prudential considerations; a woman with a track-record of abandoning her husband is hardly likely to be more faithful the second time around. And few men are eager to support another man's children financially. Women frequently express indignation at their inability to find a replacement for the husband they walked out on: I call them the angry adulteresses.

Vanity, parasitism, paranoia and infidelity are only a few of the unpleasant characteristics of contemporary western womanhood; one more is rudeness. To an extent this is part of the general decline in civility over the past half century, in which both sexes have participated. But I believe some of it is a consequence of female sexual utopianism. Here is why.

One would get the idea looking at *Cosmopolitan* magazine covers that women were obsessed with giving men sexual pleasure. This would come as news to many men. Indeed, the contrast between what women read and their actual behavior towards men has become almost surreal. The key to the mystery is that the man the *Cosmo*-girl is interested in pleasing is imaginary. He is the affluent fellow with movie star looks who is going to fall for her after one more new makeover, after she loses five more pounds or finds the perfect hairdo. In the meantime, she is free to treat the flesh-and-blood men she runs into like dirt. Why make the effort of being civil to ordinary men as long as you are certain a perfect one is going to come along tomorrow? Men of the older generation are insufficiently aware how uncouth women have become. I came rather late to the realization that the behavior I was observing in women could not possibly be normal – that if women had behaved this way in times past, the human race would have died out.

The reader who suspects me of exaggerating is urged to

spend a little time browsing women's self-descriptions on internet dating sites. They *never* mention children, but almost always manage to include the word "fun." "I like to party and have fun! I like to drink, hang out with cool people and go shopping!" The young women invite "hot guys" to contact them. No doubt some will. But would any sensible man, "hot" or otherwise, want to start a family with such a creature?

A good wife does not simply happen. Girls were once brought up from childhood with the idea that they were going to be wives and mothers. They were taught the skills necessary to that end. A young suitor could expect a girl to know a few things about cooking and homemaking. Today, many women seem unaware that they are supposed to have something to offer a husband besides a warm body.

What happens when contemporary woman, deluded into thinking she deserves a moviestar husband, fails not only to find her ideal mate, but any mate at all? She does not blame herself for being unreasonable or gullible, of course; she blames men. A whole literary genre has emerged to pander to female anger with the opposite sex. Here are a few titles, all currently available through Amazon.com: *Why Men Are Clueless, Let's Face It, Men Are @$$#%\$, How To Aggravate a Man Every Time, Things You Can Do With a Useless Man, 101 Reasons Why a Cat Is Better Than a Man, 101 Lies Men Tell Women, Men Who Hate Women and the Women Who Love Them, Kiss-off Letters to Men: Over 70 Zingers You Can Use To Send Him Packing,* or—for the woman who gets sent packing herself—*How To Heal the Hurt By Hating.*

For many women, hatred of men has clearly taken on psychotic dimensions. A large billboard in my hometown asks passing motorists: "How many women have to die before domestic violence is considered a crime?" One is forced to wonder what is going on in the minds of those who sponsor such a message. Are they really unaware that it has always been a crime for a man to murder his wife? Are they just trying to stir up fear? Or are their own minds so clouded by hatred that they can no longer view the world realistically?

This is where we have arrived after just one generation of female sexual liberation. Many men are bewildered when they realize the extent and depth of feminine rage at them. What could be making the most affluent and pampered women in history so furious?

Internet scribe Henry Makow has put forward the most plausible diagnosis I have yet seen, in an essay entitled "The Effect of Sexual Deprivation on Women."[8] *A propos* of the recent rape hysteria, he suggests: "men are 'rapists' because they are not giving women the love they need." In other words, what if the problem is that men, ahem, *aren't* preying upon women? All that we have just said supports the theory that western civilization is now facing an epidemic of female sexual frustration. And once again, the typical conservative commentator is wholly unable to confront the problem correctly: he instinctively wants to step forward in shining armor and exclaim "never fear, tender maids, I shall prevent these vicious beasts from sullying your virgin purity." If women need love from men and aren't getting it, this is hardly going to help them.

THE FORGOTTEN MEN

The attempt to realize a sexual utopia for women was doomed to failure before it began. Women's wishes aim at the impossible, conflict with one another, and change unpredictably. Hence, any program to force men (or "society") to fulfill women's wishes must fail, even if all men were willing to submit to it. Pile entitlement upon entitlement for women, heap punishment after punishment onto men: it cannot work, because women's wishes will always outpace legislation and lead to new demands.

But, while the revolution has not achieved its aims, it has certainly achieved *something*. It has destroyed monogamy and family stability. It has resulted in a polygamous mating pattern of immodest women aggressively pursuing a small number of men. It has decreased the number of children born, and insured that many who are born grow up without a father in their lives. And, least often mentioned, it has made it impossible for many decent men to find wives.

---

[8] July 7, 2003, http://www.savethemales.ca/000177.html.

One occasionally hears of surveys reporting that men are happier with their "sex lives" than women. It has always struck me as ludicrous that anyone would take this at face value. First, women are more apt than men to complain about *everything*. But second, many men (especially young men) experience a powerful *mauvaise honte* when they are unsuccessful with women. They rarely compare notes with other men, and still more rarely do so honestly. Everyone puts up a brave front, however lonely he may actually be. Hence, men almost always imagine other men to have greater success with women than is actually the case. This situation has worsened since the nineteen-sixties, with the propagation of the illusion that there is "more sex" available to men than formerly.

But if women are only mating with a few exceptionally attractive men, and if many women fail to mate at all, there *must* be a large number of men unable to get a woman. We might, in the spirit of William Graham Sumner, term them the forgotten men of the sexual revolution. I have reason to believe that a growing number are willing to come out of the closet (to use a currently popular expression) and admit that, whoever has been doing all the "hooking up" one reads about, it hasn't been them. Simple prudence dictates that we give some consideration to the situation of these men. In societies where polygamy is openly practiced (e.g., in Africa and the Muslim world), young bachelors tend to form gangs which engage in antisocial behavior: "it is not good for man to be alone."

In our society, a definite pattern has already emerged of "singles" groups or events being composed of innocent, never-married men in their thirties and cynical, bitter, often divorced women. What have the bachelors been doing with themselves all these years? So far, in the West, they have not been forming criminal gangs. (They would probably be more attractive to women if they did: everyone seems to have heard stories about men on death row being besieged with offers of marriage from bored, thrill-seeking females.)

I suggest that today's bachelors are hardly different from men who, before the sexual revolution, married young and raised families.

Natural instinct makes young men almost literally "crazy" about girls. They have a far higher regard for young women than the facts warrant. The male sex drive that modern women complain about so much exists largely for their benefit. As Schopenhauer wrote:

> Nature has provided [the girl] with superabundant beauty and charm for a few years . . . so that during these years she may so capture the imagination of a man that he is carried away into undertaking to support her honorably in some form or another for the rest of her life, a step he would seem hardly likely to take for purely rational considerations. Thus nature has equipped women, as it has all its creatures, with the tools and weapons she needs for securing her existence.[9]

I do not see any reason why young men should be less naïve about young women than they used to be.

Furthermore, many men assume women value honest, clean-living, responsible men (as opposed, e.g., to death-row criminals). So slowly, patiently, by dint of much hard work, amid uncertainty and self-doubt, our bachelor makes a decent life for himself. No woman is there to give him love, moral support, loyalty. If he did make any effort to get a wife, he may have found himself accused of harassment or stalking.

Kick a friendly dog often enough and eventually you have a mean dog on your hands.

What were our bachelor's female contemporaries doing all those years while he was an impoverished, lonely stripling who found them intensely desirable? Fornicating with dashing fellows who mysteriously declined to "commit," marrying and walking out on their husbands, or holding out for perfection. Now, lo and behold, these women, with their youthful looks gone and rapidly approaching menopause, are willing to go out with him. If they are satisfied with the free meals and enter-

---

[9] Arthur Schopenhauer, "On Women," in *Essays and Aphorisms*, trans. R. J. Hollingdale (New York: Penguin Books, 1970).

tainment he provides, he may be permitted to fork over a wedding ring. Then they will graciously allow him to support them and the children they had by another man for the rest of his life. (I have seen a woman's personal ad stating her goal of "achieving financial security for myself and my daughters.") Why in heaven's name would any man sign up for this? As one man put it to me: "if the kitten didn't want me, I don't want the cat."

Western woman has become the new "white man's burden," and the signs are that he is beginning to throw it off.

SEXUAL THERMIDOR: THE MARRIAGE STRIKE

The term Thermidor originally designated the month of the French Revolutionary calendar in which the terror ended. By July 1794, twenty or thirty persons were being guillotined daily in Paris under a so-called Law of Suspects requiring no serious evidence against the accused. Addressing the Convention on the 26th, Robespierre incautiously let slip that certain delegates were themselves under suspicion of being "traitors," but declined to name them. His hearers realized their only hope of safety lay in destroying Robespierre before he could destroy them. They concerted their plans that night, and the following morning he was arrested. Within two days, he and eighty of his followers went to the guillotine. Over the next few weeks, the prisons emptied and life again assumed a semblance of normality.

Something analogous appears to be happening today in the case of feminism. Consider, for example, the sexual harassment movement. As it spreads, the number of men who have *not* been accused steadily diminishes. Eventually a point is reached where initially sympathetic men understand that they themselves are no longer safe, that their innocence does not protect them or their jobs. Anecdotal evidence suggests that this point is being reached in many workplaces. Men are developing a self-defensive code of avoiding all unnecessary words or contact with women. One hears stories about women entering breakrooms full of merrily chatting male coworkers who look up and instantly lapse into tense, stony silence. A "hostile work environment" indeed.

A more serious development, however, is what has come to be known as the marriage strike. The first occurrence of this term appears to have been in a *Philadelphia Enquirer* editorial of 2002.[10] Two years later, a formal study gave substance to the idea: fully 22% of American bachelors aged 25-34 have resolved never to marry. 53% more say they are not interested in marrying any time soon.[11] That leaves just 25% looking for wives. This may be a situation unprecedented in the history of the world.

Some men do cite the availability of sex outside marriage as a reason for not marrying. But this does not mean that the problem could be solved simply by getting them to take vows (e.g., by shotgun marriage). Men now realize they stand to lose their children at a moment's notice through no fault of their own when the mother decides to cash out of the marriage or "relationship" in Family Court. For this reason, many are refusing to father children *with or without* benefit of clergy. In Germany, which faces an even lower birthrate than America, the talk is already of a *Zeugungsstreik*,[12] literally a "procreation-strike," rather than a mere marriage strike. Some women suffering from what has come to be known as "babies-rabies" have resorted to lying to their men about using birth-control. Of course, men are wising up to this as well.

No woman is *owed* economic support, children, respect or love. The woman who accepts and lives by correct principles thereby earns the right to make certain demands upon her husband; being female entitles her to nothing.

Western women have been biting the hand that feeds them for several decades now. It seems to me fair to say that the majority have willfully forfeited the privilege of marrying decent men. It is time for men to abandon the protector role and tell them they are going to be "liberated" from us whether they

---

[10] Dianna Thompson and Glenn Sacks, "A 'Marriage Strike' Emerges As Men Decide Not to Risk Loss," *Philadelphia Enquirer*, July 5, 2002.

[11] Barbara Defoe Whitehead and David Popenoe, *The Marrying Kind: Which Men Marry and Why* (Piscataway, N.J.: Rutgers University National Marriage Project, 2004).

[12] Title of a book by journalist Meike Dinklage, *Der Zeugungsstreik: Warum die Kinderfrage Männersache ist* (Munich.: Diana, 2005).

wish it or not. They can hold down their own jobs, pay their own bills, live, grow old and finally die by themselves. Every step which has brought them to this pass has involved an assertion of "rights" for themselves and male concessions to them. Men would seem justified in saying to them, not without a certain *Schadenfreude*, "you made your bed, now you can lie in it— alone."

Unfortunately, the matter cannot simply be allowed to rest here. Without children, the race has no future, and without women men cannot have children.

One well-established trend is the search for foreign wives. Predictably, efforts are underway by feminists to outlaw, or at least discourage this, and one law has already gotten through Congress (the International Marriage Broker Regulation Act of 2005). The ostensible reason is to protect innocent foreign lasses from "abuse"; the real reason to protect spoiled, feminist-indoctrinated American women from foreign competition. Most of the economic arguments about protective tariffs for domestic industry apply here.

Feminists think in terms of governmental coercion. The idea of *eliciting* desirable male behavior does not occur to them. Some men are concerned that proposals for forced marriage may be in the offing.

Meanwhile, men have begun to realize that any sexual intimacy with a woman can lead to date rape charges based upon things that go on in her mind afterwards, and over which he has no control. Women do frequently attempt to evade responsibility for their sexual conduct by ascribing it to the men involved. Without any social or legal enforcement of marriage, this leaves chastity as a man's only means of self-defense.

A male sex strike was probably beyond the imagination even of Aristophanes. But it may be a mistake to underestimate men. We, and not women, have been the builders, sustainers and defenders of civilization.

The latest word from college campuses is that women have begun to complain men are not asking them out. That's right: men at their hormonal peak are going to class side by side with nubile young women who now outnumber them, and are simply ignoring or shunning them. Some report being repeatedly asked "are you gay?" by frustrated coeds. This is what happens when women complain for forty years about being used as sex objects: eventually men stop using them as sex objects.

Not long ago I spotted a feminist recruitment poster at a local college. Most of it consisted of the word **FALSE** in bold capitals, visible from a distance. Underneath was something to the effect: ". . . that we're all man-hating maniacs," etc.; "come join us and see."

When the most inspiring slogan a movement can come up with amounts to "we're not as bad as everyone says," you know it is in trouble.

WHAT IS TO BE DONE?

We have arrived at a rare historical moment when we men have the upper hand in the battle of the sexes. Much depends upon the use we make of it. The only thing still propping up the present feminist-bureaucratic regime is the continued willingness of many of the hated "heterosexual white males" to live according to the old rules: not only to work, save, pay taxes and obey the law, but also to sire and raise children. Once we stop doing these things, the whole system of patronage and parasitism collapses.

My greatest fear is that at the first female concessions, the male protective instinct will kick in once again and men will cheerfully shout "all is forgiven" in a stampede to the altar. This must not happen. Our first priority must be to put the divorce industry out of business. A man must insist on nothing less than a legally binding promise to love, honor and obey him before "consenting" to give a woman a baby.

One proposal for strengthening marriage is the recognition of personalized marriage contracts. These could be made to accord with various religious traditions. I see no reason they might not stipulate that the husband would vote on behalf of his family. Feminists who think political participation more important than family life could still live as they please, but they would be forced to make a clear choice. This would help erode the superstitious belief in a universal right to participate in politics, and political life itself would be less affected by the feminine tendencies to value security over freedom and to base public policies on sentiment. Property would also be more secure where the producers of wealth have greater political power.

Economic policy should be determined by the imperative to carry on our race and civilization. There is something wrong when everyone can afford a high-definition plasma TV with three-hundred channels but an honest man of average abilities with a willingness to work cannot afford to raise a family.

Female mate selection has always had an economic aspect. Hesiod warned his male listeners in the seventh century BC that "hateful poverty they will not share, but only luxury." This notorious facet of the female sexual instinct is the reason behind the words "for richer or for poorer" in the Christian marriage ceremony. The man must know he has a solid bargain whether or not he is as successful a provider as his wife (or he himself) might like.

Within the family, the provider must control the allotment of his wealth. The traditional community of property in a marriage, i.e., the wife's claim to support from her husband, should again be made conditional on her *being* a wife to him. She may run off with the milkman if she wishes—leaving her children behind, of course (a woman willing to do this is perhaps an unfit mother in any case); but she may not evict her husband from his own house and *replace* him with the milkman, nor continue to extract resources from the husband she has abandoned. Until sensible reforms are instituted, men must refuse to leave themselves prey to a criminal regime which forces them to subsidize their own cuckolding and the abduction of their children.

The date rape issue can be solved overnight by restoring shotgun marriage—but with the shotgun at the woman's back. The "victim" should be told to get into the kitchen and fix supper for her new lord and master. Not exactly a match made in heaven, but at least the baby will have both a father and a mother. Furthermore, after the birth of her child, the woman will have more important things to worry about than whether the act by which she conceived it accorded with some women's studies professor's newfangled notion of "true consent." Motherhood has always been the best remedy for female narcissism.

Harassment accusations should be a matter of public record. This would make it possible to maintain lists of women with a history of making such charges for the benefit of employers and, far more importantly, potential suitors. Women might eventually reacquaint themselves with the old-fashioned idea that they have a reputation to protect.

Universal coeducation should be abandoned. One problem in relations between the sexes today is overfamiliarity. Young men are wont to assume that being around girls all the time will increase their chances of getting one. But familiarity is often the enemy of intimacy. When a girl only gets to socialize with young men at a dance once a week, she values the company of young men more highly. It works to the man's advantage not to be constantly in their company. Men, also, are most likely to marry when they do not understand women too well.

It is necessary to act quickly. It took us half a century to get into our present mess, but we do not have that long to get out of it. A single-generation *Zeugungsstreik* will destroy us. So we cannot wait for women to come to their senses; we must take charge and begin the painful process of unspoiling them.

HOW MONOGAMY WORKS

Traditionally, a man has been expected to marry. Bachelorhood was positively forbidden in some ancient European societies, including the early Roman Republic. Others offered higher social status for husbands and relative disgrace for bachelors. There seems to have been a fear that the sexual instinct alone was inadequate to insure a sufficient number of offspring. Another seldom mentioned motive for the expectation of marriage was husbands' envy of bachelors: "why should that fellow be free and happy when I am stuck working my life away to support an ungrateful creature who nags me?"

Strange as it sounds to modern ears, the Christian endorsement of celibacy was a liberalization of sexual morality; it recognized there could be legitimate motives for remaining unmarried. One social function of the celibate religious orders was to give that minority of men and women unsuited for or disinclined to marriage a socially acceptable way of avoiding it.

Obviously, an obligation of marrying implies the possibility of doing so. It was not difficult for an ordinary man to get a wife in times past. One reason is what I call the grandmother effect.

Civilization has been defined as the partial victory of age over youth. After several decades of married life, a woman looks back and finds it inconceivable that she once considered a man's facial features an important factor in mate selection. She tries to talk some sense into her granddaughter before it is too late. "Don't worry about what he looks like; don't worry about how he makes you feel; that isn't important." If the girl had a not especially glamorous but otherwise unexceptionable suitor (the sort who would be charged with harassment today), she might take the young man's part: "if you don't catch this fellow while you can, some smarter girl will." So it went, generation after generation. This created a healthy sense of competition for decent, as opposed to merely sexually attractive, men. Husbands often never suspected the grandmother effect, living out their lives in the comforting delusion that their wives married them solely from recognition of their outstanding merits. But today grandma has been replaced by *Cosmopolitan*, we are living with the results.

Much confusion has been caused by attempting to get women to say what it is they want from men. Usually they bleat something about "a sensitive man with a good sense of humor." But this is continually belied by their behavior. Any man who believes it is in for years of frustration and heartbreak. What they actually look for when left to their own devices (i.e., without any grandmother effect) is a handsome, socially dominant or wealthy man. Many prefer married men or philanderers; a few actively seek out criminals.

In a deeper sense, though, humans necessarily want happiness, as the philosopher says. During most of history no one tried to figure out what young women wanted; they were simply told what they wanted, viz., a good husband. This was the correct approach. Sex is too important a matter to be left to the independent judgment of young women, because young women rarely possess good judgment. The overwhelming majority of women will be happier in the long run by marrying an ordinary man and having children than by seeking sexual thrills, ascending the corporate heights or grinding out turgid tracts on gender theory. A woman develops an emotional bond with her mate through the sexual act itself; this is why arranged marriages (contrary to Western prejudice) are often reasonably happy. Romantic courtship has its charms, but is finally dispensable; marriage is not dispensable.

Finally, heterosexual monogamy is incompatible with equality of the sexes. A wife always has more influence on home life, if only because she spends more time there; a husband's leadership often amounts to little more than an occasional veto upon some of his wife's decisions. But such leadership is necessary to accommodate female hypergamy. Women want a man they can look up to; they leave or fall out of love with men they do not respect. Hence, men really have no choice in the matter.

Once more, we find nearly perfect agreement between feminist radicals and plenty of conservatives in failing to understand this, with men getting the blame from both sides. Feminists protest that "power differentials" between the sexes—meaning, really, differences in status or authority—make genuine sexual consent impossible. In a similar vein, the stern editor of *Chronicles* laments that "in the case of a college professor who sleeps with an 18-year old student, disparity in age or rank should be grounds for regarding the professor as a rapist. But professors who prey upon girls are not sent to jail. They do not even lose their jobs."[13]

In fact, this is just one more example of hypergamous female mate selection. In most marriages, the husband is at least slightly older than the wife. Normal women tend to be attracted precisely to men in positions of authority. Nurses do tend to choose doctors, secretaries their bosses, and the occasional female student will choose a professor; this does not mean the men are abusing any "power" to force helpless creatures to mate with them.

---

[13] "Anarcho-Tyranny, Rockford Style," *Chronicles* (April 2005), 44–45.

I submit that a man's "preying upon" a younger women of lower rank should be grounds for regarding him as a husband. Men are supposed to have authority over women; that is part of what a marriage is. Equality of the sexes makes men less attractive to women; it has probably contributed significantly to the decline in Western birthrates. It is time to put an end to it.

CONCLUSION

Marriage *is* an institution; it places artificial limits on women's choices. To repeat: nature dictates that males display and females choose. Monogamy artificially strengthens the male's position by insisting that (1) each female must choose a different male; and (2) each female must stick to her choice. Monogamy entails that highly attractive men are removed from the mating pool early, usually by the most attractive women. The next women are compelled to choose a less attractive mate if they wish to mate at all. Even the last and least of the females can, however, find a mate: for every girl there *is* a boy. Abolishing marriage only strengthens the naturally stronger: it strengthens the female at the expense of the male and the attractive at the expense of the unattractive.

Marriage, like most useful things, was probably invented by men: partly to keep the social peace, partly so they could be certain their wives' children were also their own. The consequences of marriage must have appeared soon after its institution: the efforts previously spent fighting over mates were replaced by strenuous exertions to provide for, rear and defend offspring. No doubt surrounding tribes wondered why one of their neighbors had recently grown so much stronger. When they learned the reason, imitation must have seemed a matter of survival.

It was, and it still is. If the Occident does not restore marriage, we will be overwhelmed by those who continue to practice it.

The Occidental Quarterly, vol. 6, no. 2 (Summer 2006): 9–37

ROTATING POLYANDRY — & ITS ENFORCERS

Michelle Langley
Women's Infidelity: Living In Limbo.
St. Louis: McCarlan Publishing, 2005

Stephen Baskerville
Taken into Custody: The War Against Fatherhood, Marriage, and the Family.
Nashville: Cumberland House Publishing, 2007

Michelle Langley's *Women's Infidelity* is probably the first book ever reviewed in *The Occidental Quarterly* advertised as "shipped in a plain envelope without any mention of the contents on the package." But even if you are not an adulterous wife yourself, there are good reasons for paying attention to Langley's documentation of social dissolution. An advanced civilization requires high-investment parenting to maintain itself. The greatest threat to proper parenting in our time is divorce, overwhelmingly initiated by the wife (70–75 percent of the time, according to Langley).

Her book's central thesis is an unpopular one: *women are no more "naturally" monogamous than men.*

Biochemical research points to a natural four-year sexual cycle for the human female. This apparently allows enough time after childbirth for the average mother in a state of savagery to regain her ability to survive without male provisioning. In the absence of any system of marriage, a woman's natural tendency is to "liberate" herself from her mate after that point. When her hormones prompt her to reproduce again, she simply takes a new mate.

Langley cites Helen Fisher's *Anatomy of Love* and Burnham and Phelan's *Mean Genes* in support of this account. According to the latter, separation and divorce are most likely to occur in the fourth year of marriage "across more than sixty radically different cultures."

Feral female sexual behavior is governed by a number of chemicals. The euphoria of infatuation is associated with the stimulant phenylethylamine, naturally produced in the body by erotic attraction. As with other drugs, it is addictive, and people gradually build up a tolerance to it, requiring ever-greater levels to achieve the same effect. Over time, it loses its power over us, and infatuation is replaced by a calm feeling of attachment to our mates. There are neurochemical factors at work here as well. But the feeling of attachment or bondedness is akin to the effect of a sedative or narcotic rather than a stimulant.

Next there are hormones to consider. The sex drive, in both men and women, is linked to testosterone levels. These are, of course, always higher in men; but the difference is greatest in early adulthood when people have traditionally taken their mates. As men age, their testosterone levels gradually decrease; women's levels rise. Going into their thirties, women get hairier, their voices deepen, and they behave more assertively. And, in the author's words, "it's also quite common for them to experience a dramatic increase in their desire for other men." (Langley cites Theresa Crenshaw's *The Alchemy of Love and Lust* and Michael Liebowitz's *The Chemistry of Love* on these matters.)

The author is not a professional researcher in any of these fields herself. She relates that, after four years of happy marriage and shortly after her 27th birthday, she began to feel bored and unhappy for no apparent reason. She turned to a number of books and professionals, all of whom agreed that the fault lay with her husband; she adopted this now conventional view for a time herself. Fortunately—and unlike most women—she kept digging for answers. She met women, at first accidentally, who described similar experiences, and questioned them. Later she began seeking women out for lengthy interviews. She eventually interviewed men as well. It is worth noting that she managed to devote several hours a week to this research without any degree in sociology or taxpayer-funded grants. Gradually, consistent patterns began to emerge from the stories she was hearing. "By the time I stopped counting, I had interviewed 123 women and 72 men. . . . I found it fascinating that something so prevalent could be kept so secret."

What, then, did she learn? First, women are more likely than men to confuse sexual attraction with love. The sexes speak differently of the feelings associated with the early stages of a romantic affair:

> Most men I have talked to call it infatuation, but most of the women I have talked to call it being in love. . . . Women in particular may believe that, if they find the right person, intense feelings can last. They've been taught to believe that they should only want sex with someone they love. So when a woman desires a man, she thinks she is in love, and when the desire fades she thinks she is out of love.

Women often speak of seeking "commitment" from men, but this would seem to imply a preference for marriage-minded men over others. Langley observed the very opposite tendency in her interviewees:

> They often form relationships with men who are emotionally inaccessible. Instead of choosing men who are interested in developing a relationship, these women choose men who make them feel insecure. Insecurity can create motivation and excitement. Women who seek excitement in their marriages (and many do) will often forego the possibility of real relationships for the excitement of fantasy relationships. . . . It's not uncommon for women to pine for men who shy away from commitment, while they shun the attention given to them by men who are willing and ready to make a commitment.

Much uninformed and superficial commentary on the sexual revolution assumes that "men want sex while women want marriage." Langley draws a valid distinction: women want to get married, not to be married. They often love not so much their husbands as their bridal-fantasy in which the man serves as a necessary prop.

Females want to wear the dress and have the wedding. Many women have looked forward to that day their whole lives, which ultimately sets them up for a huge crash.

Most women are happiest when focused on fulfilling some part of the get-married-and-live-happily-ever-after fantasy. They are content, even in relatively unfulfilling relationships, as long as some part of the fantasy is left to play out. . . .

When a woman wants to get married, she will usually overlook a lot, and at times allow herself to be treated pretty badly. After she gets married, not only is the excitement of pursuit over, after a few years of marriage the attraction buzz has dissipated too. At that point, many women may find that marriage hasn't even come close to meeting their expectations. Some women feel stupid for having wanted it so badly in the first place.

Men being pressured for "commitment" sometimes attempt to point this out: "Why is it such a big deal? What is going to be different after we're married?" The men are right, of course: a wedding ceremony has no magical power to produce lifelong happiness. Unfortunately, this seems to be something women only learn from experience.

One thing that usually does change after the wedding is the woman's willingness to overlook her man's faults. Many men will tell you: "when my wife and I were dating, I could do no wrong; now that we are married, I can do no right." Indeed, says our author, women who have tolerated their men's shortcomings and tried to please them only in pursuit of their own fantasy often enter marriage carrying a great deal of repressed anger, which usually emerges in time. The husband, for his part, feels like the victim of a "bait and switch" sales tactic. One wonders what would become of the human race if women told their boyfriends flat out: "you must marry me so I can stop pretending to love you as you are, and start complaining about all the ways you disappoint me."

Langley distinguishes, based upon her interviews, four typical stages in marital breakdown.

(1) The wives begin to feel vaguely that "something is missing in their lives." Then they experience a loss of interest in sexual relations with their husbands. The author is clear that her interviewees were *not* being "abused" or mistreated in any way. Nevertheless, in some cases "the women claimed that when their husbands touched them, they felt violated; they said their bodies would freeze up and they would feel tightness in their chest and/or a sick feeling in their stomach."

(2) After a certain interval, they experience an unexpected reawakening of sexual desire—but not, alas, for their lawful husbands. In many cases, the women did not act upon their new desires quickly. Usually they would go through a period of feeling guilty, and sometimes try to assuage these feelings by increased attentiveness toward their husbands.

Women, says Langley, enter marriage assuming they are naturally monogamous. "*Trying* to be faithful doesn't seem natural to them." They recite the wedding vow in much the same spirit as they wear "something borrowed, something blue"—it is simply what one does at a wedding. Of course, a vow is no very serious undertaking to one who assumes she will never feel any temptation to break it.

Accordingly, over time, most women begin to rationalize their extramarital erotic interests. If women simply want to be married and are not naturally inclined to be attracted to other men, "any unhappiness or infidelity on the part of the women is assumed to be due to the men they married." This seems to me a critically important and easily overlooked finding: the widely propagated notion that women are naturally monogamous is helping to nourish the contemporary "blame the man for everything" mentality. Hence, odd as this sounds, in order to reestablish the actual practice of monogamy, it may be necessary to discredit the notion that woman are naturally inclined to it.

Once women start believing their wayward desires can be blamed upon their husbands' failures, they become "negative and sarcastic when speaking about their husbands and their marriages." It is then usually just a matter of time and opportunity before the wives proceed to actual adultery.

(3) Women involved in extramarital affairs speak of "feelings unlike anything they'd experienced before. They felt 'alive' again." This euphoria was, however, combined with pain and guilt. Often before a tryst, they would vow that "this would be the last time," but were unable to keep their resolutions. The author interprets this as addictive behavior related to the brain chemistry of erotic attachment. She conjectures that the "high" produced by adultery is more intense than that of lawful courtship because of its association with shame, guilt and secrecy: a plausible hypothesis, and possible topic for future research.

Usually the women did not act decisively to end their marriages, which gave them a sense of security in spite of everything. Divorce produces separation anxiety, which is a sort of chemical withdrawal. Habitual attachments produce a safe, comfortable feeling, like a sedative; and loss of a person to whom we are bonded produces a panicky feeling like that of a child lost in a department store, Langley writes. So these women often lived in a "state of limbo" for years, unable to decide whether to remain married or seek a divorce. Most expected they would eventually achieve clarity about their own desires, but this seldom happened. The author's hypothesis is that "clarity never comes, because what they are really trying to do is avoid pain. They are hoping that one day it won't hurt to leave their spouse, or that one day they'll no longer desire to be with someone else and will want to return to their spouse." (She neglects to mention that it may "hurt" many women to renounce their husbands' financial support as well.)

Sometimes the paramour breaks off relations with the adulterous wife, for any number of reasons. In these cases, the women "experienced extreme grief, became deeply depressed and expressed tremendous anger *toward their husbands*" (my emphasis). In fact, according to Langley's hypothesis, they were experiencing another form of withdrawal—they were stimulant addicts forced to go "cold turkey." These women "placed the utmost importance on finding a relationship that gave them the feeling they experienced in their affairs. In the meantime, "some women resumed sporadic sexual relations with their husbands in an effort to safeguard the marriage." Though no longer attracted to their husbands, "desire was temporarily rekindled when they suspected their husbands were unfaithful [or] showed signs of moving on." In other words, even wives who have been unfaithful for years want to keep their husbands hanging on — they do not want *him* to leave *them.*

(4) Finally some women do reach a sort of resolution. This may mean divorce or a decision to remain married and continue their affairs indefinitely. *Langley does not mention a single case in which an adulterous wife returned to her husband unreservedly and sincerely.* Those who divorced and remarried sometimes expressed "regret for having hurt their children and ex-spouses only to find themselves experiencing similar feelings in the new relationship." In other words, they had reached the end of a second feral sexual cycle, and boredom had returned. The "natural" female sex drive results in rotating polyandry. Langley even entitles one chapter "The Commitment Game: Female Version of Pursue and Discard." One can hardly avoid the thought that these women might have saved everyone a lot of trouble by simply keeping their original marriage vow.

Like other observers of the contemporary scene, the author notes the pervasiveness of female anger. "It's impossible . . . to understand anything about women in this country today, unless you understand that a) they're angry, and b) their anger is directed at men. Women today aren't seeking equality. They want retribution — revenge."

Much of this is due to feminist indoctrination. An ideological regime (and feminism may now, I think, legitimately be called a regime) paints the past in the darkest colors possible in order to camouflage its own failures. According to official "herstory," women's lives were a virtual hell on earth before the glorious dawn of feminism. They were beaten and brutalized, burned as witches, forcibly prevented from acquiring the education for which they were supposedly thirsting. Theologians allegedly taught that they had no souls. Unfortunately, Langley appears to accept at least some of this balderdash: "When women decide to leave their husbands, all the pain from their past *together with all the pain women have suffered at the hands of men throughout history* is unleashed on their husbands in the form of anger, regardless of whether or not their husbands have treated them badly" (my emphasis).

Langley is on firmer ground when she suggests women actually enjoy being angry because it gives them a kind of power: "Angry people not only spur those around them to walk on eggshells, they motivate them to do exactly what the angry person wants them to do. Some women stay angry long after divorcing their husbands because, as long as they're angry and their ex-husbands feel guilty, they've got power over them."

A third factor is the unrealistic expectations women now have about marriage: "their not getting the expected payoff [of] continued excitement over getting and being married."

It should also be pointed out that the very terms "retribution" and "revenge" imply that husbands have wronged their wives somehow. If this is not the case, and Langley admits that today it mostly is not, the proper terms for the women's behavior would be "wanton cruelty" or "sadism." This supposition is strengthened by some of the author's own observations: "I've noticed that once a woman reaches a certain point, not only does her anger persist, she wants to continually punish and inflict pain on whomever has angered her. . . . The men that I talked to often used the word *evil* to describe the behavior of their wives."

Let us consider the author's male interviewees and their reactions to these patterns of female behavior. Langley lists three obstacles to male recognition of the reality of female infidelity: (1) a kind of high-minded attitude that "*my* wife simply isn't 'that kind' of woman," which usually amounts to wishful thinking; (2) an invalid inference from the wife's lack of interest in sexual relations with *them* to a lack of sexual interests generally; and (3) a failure to discuss and compare notes on marital problems with other men, as women routinely do with one another.

The author emphasizes the gullibility of the men she interviewed. One man's wife had walked out on him and rented an apartment; three years later, he still had no suspicions that she might be with another man. Often the wives who took advantage of their husbands' credulousness were highly jealous themselves: "Some of the husbands learned to look down in restaurants and other public places, because they feared their wife would accuse them of looking at another woman. Some claimed that their wife didn't want them to watch certain television programs." Psychologists call this projection: the automatic attribution of one's own thoughts and motivations to others. Thus, dishonorable women tend to be suspicious; faithful husbands are trusting.

In the author's experience, however, men do not get much credit with their wives for placing so much trust in them:

> Some of the women resented their husbands' lack of suspicion. . . . Although females never give males any indication that they are anything less than 100 percent faithful, [they] seem to think men are stupid for believing them. Females just think males should know that when they say "I would never cheat on you," what they really mean is "I would never cheat on you . . . as long as you make me happy and I don't get bored."

Of course, if men did know this, it is unlikely many of them would want to get married.

Women may want men to make them happy, but they do not say, and probably do not know themselves, how this might be accomplished. "Women want men to read their minds — or, more accurately, their emotions — because it's what they do, easily. . . . Females want males to anticipate their needs and desires." (Obeying their every command is not enough.) Women do in fact have a greater ability to perceive the needs and feelings of others without verbal communication, an evolved adaptation to the requirements of successfully nurturing infants. When they expect their husbands to have this same ability, they are in effect upset that their husbands are not women.

Eventually, women do come out and tell their husbands they are "unhappy." But this does not mean they have any intention of working on improving the marriage; women ordinarily make no overt, specific complaints until they are

> 100 percent done with the relationship — meaning [they] have lost all feeling. . . . It's not uncommon for women to

eventually feel less for their husbands than they would for
a stranger on the street. . . . When women start being specific to men about their needs, it's usually only to let their
husbands know all the many areas in which they have
failed. In other words, their husbands have already been
fired; their wives are just giving them the reasons for the
termination. . . . She already has another "Mr. Right"
picked out or is eager to find one. She is looking for the
feeling of excitement again.

Men rarely understand this. The author found that most men
blamed themselves and "beat themselves up" for the things they
thought they had done wrong in the marriage. Their initial response to their wives' stated unhappiness was to *try to make them
happy*. "In most cases, their husbands launched futile attempts to
make their wives happy by being more attentive, spending more
time at home and helping out around the house. Regardless of
these women's past and present complaints, the last thing they
wanted was to spend more time with their husbands." (Langley
notes that wives do often complain that "my spouse doesn't pay
attention to me," but calls this code for "I want another man.")
In fact, wives often became angry precisely over their husbands'
efforts to please them, because this increased their own feelings
of guilt for infidelity. Some also perceived the similarity between
this behavior and their own earlier efforts to get their husbands
to "commit"; women know better than anyone that efforts to
please can be a form of manipulation.

The women sometimes responded with a kind of counter-
manipulation: "they thought if they were cold and treated their
husbands terribly, the men would leave, or ask them to leave."
Sometimes this happens—which, incidentally, explains why divorce initiation statistics can be misleading. A significant portion
of the roughly thirty percent of divorces which are formally
male-initiated result from the wife deliberately maneuvering her
husband into taking the step.

But it is not always easy for women to obtain a divorce in this
manner: "Some of the women couldn't believe the things their
husbands were willing to put up with." (So much for men not

being committed.) The author recounts cases where women deliberately tried to provoke their husbands into striking them because they calculated it would be to their advantage in the looming child-custody dispute. One reason husbands may be so difficult to provoke today is that they realize the only result will be a jail term for "domestic abuse" or a restraining order preventing them from seeing their children.

> Most of the men didn't have anyone to talk to other than their wives, which is why I believe they tried so desperately to hold on to them. . . . Some of the men were so dependent on their wives, they didn't think they could live without them, but one thing all the men shared was a fear of losing their children.
>
> The men I interviewed feared losing their family, but the women didn't seem to have that fear. The women thought of it as losing their husbands, not their family. More often than not, the men were forced to move out of their homes and away from their kids. They lost all of their attachment bonds and felt as though they were losing their whole identity.
>
> Many of the men became suicidal when their wife left and remained so for a long time afterwards. A few of the men said that they felt homicidal.

On the other hand, "the word used by the majority of women I interviewed to describe their husbands [was] 'pathetic.'" When the full extent of their husband's emotional dependence upon them comes out, women are not moved or gratified; they feel contempt for what they see as weakness.

Sometimes another woman entered the abandoned husband's life:

> but the affairs were usually mired in the man's grief. In a few cases, the man was unable to have sexual relationships with the woman he started seeing. . . . To say they were in pain would be an understatement. . . . The men developed these relationships so they could have some-

one to talk to. Most said that having an affair was the last thing on their minds at the time, but they didn't know what else to do. They felt lonely and isolated. Many men credited the woman who helped them with saving their lives, which may be a literal truth.

What are we to make of all this?

Men have an inherent reluctance about joining together to defend their interests in the manner of feminists. One reason, I believe, is they fear it would seem *unmanly*. While feminists blather about "uncomfortable environments" like princesses fussing over peas, men learn early to swallow large amounts of pain and disappointment: this is simply part of what it means to be a man. The toughening they receive from their fathers and peer groups usually stands them in good stead. They must, after all, learn to make their own way in an unfair world that does not care about their feelings.

But all men have their limits. I do not see how any society can expect men to endure from their women the abhorrent behavior Michelle Langley describes. Reports of suicides and other violent behavior on the part of abandoned husbands denied access to their children are getting onto the internet. Despite the powerful presence of feminist gatekeepers, even the "old" news media will not be able to maintain a complete blackout forever. The "backlash" feminists have long talked about is just beginning.

The reader has probably gathered by now that *Women's Infidelity* is not the sort of book that would inspire a young man to go out and fall in love. Concerned as all of us must be about declining birthrates, I could not in good conscience urge any young man coming of age in America today to marry, or even to date. There is simply no point in continuing to play by the old rules with women who openly despise those rules. Instead, I would recommend working hard, saving money, refusing to socialize with spoiled women, and reading Michelle Langley if you want to learn what kinds of things you are missing out on. If you still cannot rid yourself of the desire to marry, learning an Eastern European language might not be a bad investment.

The reality of marriage in any age is indeed such that it has never been easy to make it a sensible choice for a man from a purely self-interested point of view. The sexual instinct and romantic illusions can only do so much. This is why it has often been necessary to exhort contented bachelors that it would be "immature and irresponsible" of them not to take a wife. Above and beyond this, dowries often used to be offered with brides to sweeten the deal. Our author's description of this ancient custom is delightful: "females are considered a worthless burden so families pay men to marry them."

Langley reports that she interviewed just two men who responded effectively to the challenge of their wives' disloyalty.

> The first man took the initiative and filed for divorce after his wife expressed on several occasions that she was unhappy and considering a separation. Before the divorce was final, his wife was trying to reconcile, but he chose not to because of her [lack of interest] in working on the marriage prior to his filing for divorce.

The second case was a man in a second marriage who had made all the usual mistakes the first time around but, unlike most husbands, managed to learn from the experience. As soon as his second wife started talking about a vague "unhappiness," he inferred that she had met another man. He put down in writing clear conditions for remaining married to her and refused to agree to any separation, knowing it would only be a prelude to divorce. Insisting she break off her extramarital affair at once, he wrote: "I will not allow my spirit to deteriorate because of your indecision." Rather than attempting to remove all possible grounds for his wife's discontent, he simply told her: "complaining is no longer acceptable. If you want me to do or not do something, you must tell me what it is. I do not expect you to read my mind and I will no longer try to read yours." This worked.

A man cannot force his wife to be faithful, but he can force her to make a clear choice; he can refuse to allow her the opportunity of having both a marriage and an affair, of continuing in a "limbo" of indecisiveness. Langley even reports that some unfaithful wives themselves "wanted their husband to give them an ultimatum—a kick in the ass, so to speak."

Delivering an ultimatum, be it noted, is incompatible with such sacred bromides as "commitment" and "unconditional love." One lesson to be drawn from *Women's Infidelity* is that husbands need to be *less* committed to their wives rather than more. Without legal enforcement of the marriage contract, the threat of abandonment seems to be the only thing that sometimes keeps women in line. Rather than fulminating against men who "love 'em and leave 'em," we might do better to hold ticker-tape parades in honor of husbands who say "enough is enough" and walk out; at least wives would have an incentive to keep their men happy. In any case, the women Langley describes hardly seem to deserve undying loyalty.

The conservative commentariat is clueless as usual about these realities. All they have to offer is empty sermonizing about the sacredness of the marriage vow and sanctimonious rubbish about men "preying upon" and abandoning supposedly weak and helpless women. This is of no help to a husband faced with the reality of an unfaithful wife and the prospect of losing his family through no fault of his own. As long as men do nothing more than keep their marriage vows to women who are trampling upon their own and abusing their husbands' trust, the situation can only continue to deteriorate.

When you destroy a fundamental social institution—and none is more fundamental than marriage—the usual result is a powerful lesson in why the institution was established in the first place. Never before have we actually been able to observe how women behave when unrestrained by honor, shame, religious instruction, or fear of social disgrace and financial ruin. In our author's words, "We are just starting to see glimpses of women's natural sexual behavior." If her stories provide the glimpses, one shudders to imagine what the full-length view will look like.

Langley is better at describing and diagnosing than at prescribing remedies. She actually concludes with the hope that her work might serve to "reduce the use of shame as a sexual deterrent for females." In other words, *women are not yet shameless enough.* In her view, the only justification for shaming women into marital fidelity in the past was to ease husbands' paternity anxiety. She believes the advent of DNA testing has rendered this aspect of traditional sexual morality obsolete. She thereby joins a long line of persons who have imagined that some technical advance — pills, latex, new abortion procedures — will allow men and women to dispense with self-control and fidelity. But this will require the cooperation of men.

How does she imagine a husband will react when his wife tells him "I am going to sleep with another man, but don't worry: we'll just have the baby DNA tested to determine the financial obligations." My guess is that husbands will be about as happy with this arrangement as wives would be with men who said "I'm going to bed with my secretary, but don't worry: I'll use a condom, so nobody will catch a disease and all my income will still go to support our children." Sexual jealousy is an evolved irrational drive inexplicable in merely prudential or economically rational terms.

Like many contemporary writers, Langley discusses sex at great length without much considering the most obvious thing about it, viz., that *it is where babies come from*. She is childless herself and nowhere considers the possibility that the vague "something missing" from the lives of bored, unhappy matrons is children.

My great-grandmother raised nine children to adulthood in a world without supermarkets, refrigerators, or washing machines. She did not have much time to search for "unconditional love" or "commitment," because she was too busy practicing it herself. Most of her life was taken up with the unceasing procurement and preparation of food for her husband and children. Yet she got along fine without romance novels, child custody gamesmanship, or psychotherapy; she was, I am told, always cheerful and contented. This is something beyond the imagination of barren, resentful feminists. It is the satisfaction which results from knowing that one is carrying out a worthwhile task to the best of one's abilities, a satisfaction nothing else in life can give. We are here today because this is the way women used to behave; we cannot continue long under the present system of rotating polyandry.

While Michelle Langley focuses on the psychology of "liberated" female sexual behavior, Stephen Baskerville's *Taken into Custody* details for us the brutal police-state machinery which has grown up in the past forty years to encourage, enforce, and profit from it. Here is the reality behind such commonplace euphemisms as "marital breakdown" and "custody disputes":

> A man comes home one day to find his house empty. On the table is a note from his wife saying she has taken the children to live with her sister or parents or boyfriend, or to a "battered women's shelter." Soon after comes a knock on the door. He is summoned to appear [at] a family court within a few hours. In a hearing that lasts a few minutes his children are legally removed from his care . . . and he is ordered to stay away from them most or all of the time. He is also ordered to begin making child support payments, an order is entered to garnish his wages, and his name is placed on a federal government database for monitoring "delinquents." If he tries to see his children outside the authorized time, or fails to make the payments, he can be arrested. Without being permitted to speak, he is told the hearing is over.
>
> The man may be accused of domestic violence or child sexual abuse, in which case there may be no hearing at all . . . but the police will simply come to the door and order him to leave his home within hours, or minutes, even if no evidence has been presented against him. . . . The man may also be ordered to pay alimony and the fees of lawyers he has not hired and threatened with arrest if he refuses or is unable. . . . If he refuses to hire a lawyer he will be ordered to pay his spouse's lawyer. Either way, he will pay $50,000–$150,000 and possibly much more. . . . If he refuses to answer questions or pay he can be jailed without a trial. . . . If he objects, he can be ordered to undergo a psychiatric evaluation.

At his "trial," he will be interrogated about the most intimate details of his family life.

And no answer is correct. If he works long hours, he is a careerist who neglects his children. If he cares for his children, he is failing to earn as much income for them as he might. If he disciplines his children, he is controlling or even abusive. If he does not, he is neglectful. If he does not bathe them, he is neglecting them. If he does, he may be molesting them.

All this costs him "$400–$500 an hour, and the ordeal lasts as long as the lawyers and judge wish to drive up the fees."

> Whatever the outcome of the trial, for the rest of his children's childhood they and he will live under constant surveillance and control by the court. He will be told when he can see his children, what he can do with them, where he can take them . . . what religious services he may (or must) attend with them and what subjects he may discuss with them in private. . . . He can be ordered to work certain hours and at certain jobs, the earnings from which will be confiscated. . . . If he loses his job or is hospitalized he will be declared a felon and jailed for failure to pay child support. His home can be entered by officials of the court. . . . His financial records will be demanded and examined by the court and his bank account will be raided. . . . His children can be compelled to act as informers against him. He can be ordered to sell his house and turn the proceeds over to attorneys he has not hired.

Baskerville notes that the very monstrousness of the injustices being committed against fathers prevents some people from accepting that they are taking place. A common initial reaction to the horror stories is "if things are really as bad as that, wouldn't we have heard about it before now?"

There are several reasons. One, of course, is that journalists whose job it is to inform us of corruption in public life prefer to entertain us with features on "gay marriage" and movie stars' romances. But a second is that the family courts directly retaliate against parents who attempt to organize or speak out. It is a crime in many jurisdictions to criticize a family court judge; where it is not, judges can simply issue individual gag orders from the bench. Baskerville reports instances of fathers who were arrested for talking to reporters about their cases. Sheriff's deputies photograph protest demonstrations by fathers' groups. Internet sites have been shut down. Archaic laws against "defamatory libel" and "scandalizing the court" have been resurrected to prosecute critics. Court officials have been deputized to monitor fathers' criticisms of the court in the press and in their private correspondence (which they can be ordered to hand over on pain of incarceration). Meanwhile, officials are free to discuss the private lives of fathers openly in public meetings and post information about their cases on the Internet.

Family court proceedings occur behind closed doors, and most often no records are kept. In cases where they are, they have sometimes been illegally falsified by unknown persons. Judges cite "family privacy" as the rational for secrecy. But in fact, the Clerk of Courts is required to make plenty of information about "defendants" (fathers) public: Social Security numbers, unlisted telephone numbers, and more. They are prohibited, however, from divulging the name of the judge assigned to the case. Baskerville draws the obvious conclusion: The purpose of all the secrecy and censorship is not to protect family privacy but to allow the courts to invade it with impunity.

A third obstacle to public recognition that innocent men are being railroaded is that fathers themselves believe the propaganda about "deadbeat dads." Even after becoming victims of the system, they assume some mistake must have been made in their particular case, while other men are the "real" deadbeats the government rightly pursues. An important factor contributing to this misapprehension is a sentimental view of motherhood and female innocence left over from an earlier age but now demonstrably at variance with the facts. One writer quoted by Baskerville reports: "All the domestic relations lawyers I spoke with concurred that *in disputes involving child custody* women initiate divorce *'almost all the time.'*" Men more often attempt to avoid divorce: "Fifty-eight percent of men delayed their divorce because of its impact on children. Far fewer women [viz., 37 percent] had this worry."

Many conservatives will no doubt agree that strong-arm methods are unwarranted against lawfully wedded and faithful fathers, but protest that they may be necessary against those scoundrels who "prey upon" women without having escorted them to an altar. Baskerville, however, cites evidence that even unwed fathers do not normally abandon their offspring:

> An American study of young, low-income, and unmarried fathers presents a picture that, while far from ideal, does not show them abandoning their children: 63% had only one child; 82% had children by only one mother . . . 70% saw their children at least once a week . . . and large percentages reported bathing, feeding, dressing and playing with their children; and 85% provided informal child support in the form of cash or purchased goods such as diapers, clothing and toys.

Another survey, conducted in the north of England, found that "the most common reason given by the fathers for not having more contact with their children was the mothers' reluctance to let them." Here we see one of the reasons for marriage: not to prevent men from absconding, but to prevent women from interfering with the father-child bond.

In other words, fatherhood is natural. If shotgun marriages and child support collection agencies were necessary to force men to provide for their offspring (as so many sanctimonious male commentators imply), civilization could never have arisen in the first place. The human male simply *cannot* be as bad as now routinely portrayed, whether by hate-filled feminists or pharisaical conservatives.

Here are just a few more highlights from Baskerville's relentless catalogue of divorce industry injustices:

A man in the United Kingdom received a sentence of ten months for greeting his child on the street.

Children have been jailed for refusal to testify against their fathers. A seventeen-year-old girl was wrestled to the ground and handcuffed by two male police detectives for refusal to leave her father's apartment.

Fathers have been kept away from the bedsides of their dying children.

Custodial parents are not answerable to anyone for use of child support payments, and need not spend any of it on the children. States use "child support" money to balance their budgets, or for any other purpose they please.

Some states have instituted "expedited judicial processes" in which fathers are summoned to appear not before judges but before "judicial commissioners" or "marital masters," essentially ordinary lawyers dressed up in judge's robes. These persons sometimes double as lobbyists for legislation relating to child support.

In Warren County, Pennsylvania, a man was threatened with prison unless he signed a preprinted confession stating "I have physically and emotionally battered my partner. . . . I am responsible for the violence I used. My behavior was not provoked."

Private companies have been dragooned into performing surveillance functions for the divorce regime. Employers are required by law to inform on all employees, including those who have never been ordered to pay child support. The information goes into a National Directory of New Hires, maintained for use against any persons who might get behind on child support in the future. This practice "annexes the personnel offices of private companies as administrative agents of the government." Efforts are underway to make similar use of churches and community organizations such as the YMCA and United Way.

Child support is demanded from men who have been proven not to be the fathers of the children in question. Women are sometimes allowed to collect full child support from more than one man.

In the U.K. and Australia, it has been proposed to outlaw home paternity testing kits available from private companies, so that men may be arrested for attempting to prove they are not the fathers of the children they have been ordered to support.

Also in Britain, feminist groups and bureaucrats can bring

domestic violence charges against men they target as abusers on the theory that the victim herself "should be spared having to take legal action." These third-party accusers do not have to provide evidence that the alleged victim even exists.

Some mothers in Massachusetts report being pressured and threatened by social service agents with the loss of their children if they refuse to divorce their husbands.

There are now moves afoot to prosecute "deadbeat accomplices," meaning parents or second wives or other relatives of child support extortionees. One second wife was charged with "harboring a fugitive." Such persons' bank accounts may be seized to pay child support for the fathers they are "abetting."

Teenage boys statutorily raped by adult women may be held liable for child support paid to those women.

In one weird case in Iowa, an eleven-year-old boy's savings (from chores such as shoveling snow) were confiscated by the state in order to pay child support for *himself*—possible since, as a minor, his father's name was also on his bank account.

Most disturbingly of all, to my mind: Fathers have been ordered to submit to something called a "plethysmograph," in which an electronic sheath is placed over the penis while they are made to view pornographic movies involving children.

Baskerville lists numerous legal guarantees violated by family courts, including several Amendments to the Constitution, the presumption of innocence, the separation of powers, *habeas corpus*, and the prohibitions against double jeopardy, *ex post facto* laws, and bills of attainder. The courts openly acknowledge that Constitutional guarantees do not apply in their proceedings—justified, it is asserted, because they are courts of "equity" rather than law. Federal courts never review cases involving family law; family courts are accountable only to review boards dominated by bar associations, i.e., by lawyers with a pecuniary interest in maximizing extortions from divorced men. Baskerville rightly notes an odd circumstance: A vast literature exists castigating the judicial branch for usurping legislative power, ignoring original intent, misapplying the Fourteenth Amendment, and various other sins; but the family court system, which has a greater influence on more people's lives, has almost entirely escaped scrutiny.

Feminist ideology certainly played a role in creating the current situation; but, as usual, more was involved than ideas having consequences. Much of the divorce industry's growth has simply been an instance of the normal tendency of bureaucrats to seek to increase their wealth and power. For most of these persons, feminism has been more pretext than motivation. The judges, indeed, "promiscuously invoke both the traditional stereotypes about motherhood and modern ideas of women's rights." Probably most have no deep convictions at all in the matter.

The same gap between rationalizing rhetoric and the reality of material interest is visible throughout the divorce industry, which consists not only of judges and lawyers, but also a bevy of "experts" — psychiatrists, psychologists, social workers, mediators, custody evaluators, visitation monitors, and instructors for mandatory "parenting education" and "anger management" classes. All are paid through forced exactions from fathers.

Psychotherapists are ubiquitous in the industry, in part because they fear insufficient demand for their services on the market. One attorney says "if you put ten psychiatrists in a room you'll get ten different opinions." Baskerville gives just one example: A father was diagnosed by one psychiatrist as having both a "dysthymic disorder" and a "mixed personality disorder," which included "obsessive-compulsive behavior, rigidity, grandiose thinking, and passive-aggressive traits"; a second psychiatrist came up with "schizotypal personality disorder" instead. Such "expert opinions" are rarely presented in open court, so there is no possibility of cross-examination, and the psychiatrists may be covered by judicial immunity, so they cannot be held accountable for their testimony. As one law professor asks: "What made all these people all of a sudden lunatics and unfit to parent?"

Obviously, the job of the expert is to provide a veneer of rationality for court decisions which are either wholly arbitrary or made on other grounds, such as maximizing the amount of money extracted from the father. If a family court does not have access to some arcane art of determining "the best interests of the child," its claim to be engaged in anything more than kidnapping collapses. (Pseudorationality of this sort is a prominent feature of managerial rule in general: Does anyone seriously believe, e.g., that corporate "diversity consultants" are in possession of some profound science the rest of us lack?) It is not altogether surprising that little training is necessary to qualify as such an "expert." Courts may appoint "persons with only undergraduate degrees or less, one or two weekend seminars or workshops, and maybe a four-hour in-service training program."

As always, the wielders of power claim the moral high ground. "Fathers almost universally report being insulted and harangued with the *obiter dicta* of judges as if they were naughty boys or juvenile delinquents," Baskerville writes. The *New York Daily News* produced a credulous report on the "parent education classes" judges now commonly order divorcing couples to attend; these are said to be necessary in order to "[t]each them how to behave; maybe even shame them into acting their age."

The author devotes twenty pages to an historical sketch of federal involvement in child support collection. It began not as a response to any widespread problem of parental abandonment but to political pressure from feminist groups and bar associations. President Ford somewhat reluctantly signed legislation creating the Office of Child Support Enforcement in 1975, warning that it was an unwarranted federal intrusion into families and the role of the states. The original rational was that the government would save on welfare payments to unmarried mothers by getting the fathers to pay more. Critics pointed out at the time that most welfare mothers did not even have child support orders, and most of the fathers were too poor in any case to pay what the mothers received in welfare benefits.

In 1988, Congress passed the Family Support Act, with two key provisions: (1) states were required to implement presumptive (and virtually compulsory) child support guidelines; and (2) the use of criminal enforcement machinery was extended from welfare cases to *all* child support orders.

Non-welfare fathers are both far more numerous and wealthier than the fathers of welfare babies originally targeted. Today, non-welfare fathers account for 83 percent of child support cases (a proportion which continues to grow) and 92 percent of the money collected. *Yet there had never been a serious problem of non-payment on the part of these men.* Since 1988, increasing revenue has been the real aim of the program, and the supposed need to force "deadbeats" to support their children has never been anything but a hoax intended to confuse the public.

Oddly, the program actually loses money at the federal level; it cost taxpayers $2.7 billion in 2002, for example, and the deficit continues to increase. This money gets paid out to state officials as an incentive to increase the amount *they* collect: The more they extort from fathers, the more the federal government rewards them, regardless of whether the men are guilty of anything. In 2002, for example, Ohio collected $228 million, while California got $640 million.

In order to receive their cut of the swag, states are *required to channel payments through their criminal enforcement machinery.* In other words, they must treat all divorced fathers, even those who pay their child support in full and on time, like criminals. And they do; officials boast of collecting so-and-so many millions of dollars "from deadbeats." Criminality is simply ascribed by the government to every divorced father.

Current child support guidelines, Baskerville reports, are largely the creation of one man, a Dr. Robert Williams. In 1987, he founded Policy Studies Inc., a "private" consulting and collection agency targeting government contracts in child support enforcement. Simultaneously, in his capacity as consultant for the Department of Health and Human Services, he drew up a set of model child support guidelines. Obviously, his business interests were best served by making the guidelines as onerous as possible. In Baskerville's words, "only by creating a level of obligation high enough to create hardship for fathers can the guidelines create a large enough pool of defaulters to ensure profits and demand for the services of his private collection agency."

It worked. The following year, as mentioned, the Family Support Act was passed, requiring states to implement their own child support guidelines in order to qualify for federal handouts, and they were given a short time in which to draw them up. Most did the easiest thing and simply adopted Williams' own guidelines endorsed by HHS. As government began whipping up "deadbeat dad" hysteria, his company's earnings soared.

A number of state courts have ruled against the guidelines. A Georgia superior court described them as "contrary to common sense," since they bear no relation to the actual costs of raising children. Furthermore, they create "a windfall to the oblige. . . . The presumptive award leaves the non-custodial parent in poverty while the custodial parent enjoys a notable higher standard of living." A Wisconsin court pointed out that the state guidelines would "result in a figure so far beyond the child's needs as to be irrational." All such rulings were reversed on government appeal.

Divorced fathers have their cars booted and their driver's and professional licenses revoked, which prevents them from getting or keeping employment. They routinely lose their houses, and many end up in homeless shelters, which one philosophically described as "better than being in jail." Baskerville cites one case of a father being hospitalized for malnutrition because he was not left enough money to feed himself adequately.

The U.S. now has a larger percentage of its population behind bars than any other nation in the world. How many of these prisoners are fathers jailed for nonpayment of child support? For some reason, the Bureau of Justice Statistics will not tell us. We do know that proposals are being made for relieving prison overcrowding by constructing special detention camps for fathers.

Public relations campaigns are being devised to put a more acceptable face upon what is happening. A Virginia enforcement director describes the fathers he pursues as "clients" and "customers" who "are entitled to have the benefit of child support services." Robert Williams's company has "customer service units . . . for fostering cooperation with each customer" and "[s]pecialized customer service centers . . . for increasing responsiveness to customers." Baskerville dryly comments: "These . . . entrepreneurs neglect to mention that customers who choose not to patronize their establishments will be arrested."

In January 2000, HHS Secretary Donna Shalala proudly announced that "federal and state child support enforcement program broke new records in nationwide collections in fiscal year 1999, reaching $15.5 billion, nearly double the amount collected in 1992." At the same time, collections have gone *down* when measured as a percentage of what the government claims fathers "owe." The reason? Interest and arrearages created by Williams's guidelines are piled up on the heads of fathers faster than actual money can be squeezed out of them. Most of this fictitious debt can never be collected, of course.

The "domestic violence" we hear so much about is essentially just another aspect of the divorce game. When a woman leaves her husband, she is routinely advised to accuse him of "abuse," whether of herself or the children. No evidence is necessary; the husband is hauled off to prison and forbidden most types of contact with his family. Courts themselves sponsor seminars on how to fabricate accusations, and there are no penalties for perjury.

Baskerville notes that the literature on "domestic violence" evinces no concern with prosecuting men directly for violent acts. Indeed, were men beating their wives, there would be no need for a special category of violence labeled "domestic"; they could simply be prosecuted for battery under the same laws that apply to other cases. The complaint of "domestic violence" activists is almost exclusively that "abusers" might retain custody or visitation rights for their children. They speak ominously of the "batterers" making "threats of kidnapping." This simply means that involuntarily divorced fathers want their children back.

It is important to note that terms such as abuse, violence, and battery do not, in the surreal world of feminism and divorce law, have their traditional English meanings. As early as 1979, feminists were writing of men who battered their wives "by ignoring [them] and by working late." Today, women are instructed that abuse includes "name-calling," "giving you negative looks," "ignoring your opinions," and (most revealingly, in my view) "refusing to let you have money." The U.S. Department of Justice has declared that "undermining an individual's sense of self-worth" is domestic violence and hence a federal crime.

The usual fate of a man charged with "abuse" is to receive a restraining order (sometimes called an order of protection). This is a decree issued from the bench without evidence being presented and without the man being summoned to speak in his own defense; it prohibits a wide range of otherwise legal behavior. It declares the man a criminal and subject to arrest should he continue to live peacefully in his own home or associate with his own children. One law professor notes that "[p]art of the reason the order exists is to be violated." Even if no evidence exists to convict him, "the protection order can provide the basis for criminal liability on the more easily proven crime of violating the order."

Restraining orders are said to be doled out "like candy" to all who apply. Fathers who contact their children are prosecuted for "stalking," an offense the government defines as any "nonconsensual communication." (Try accusing the IRS of stalking you.) Even fathers for whom child visitation rights have been established remain under restraining orders which, like tripwires, can trigger arrest for the most innocent behavior. Acts for which fathers have been charged include opening an apartment door so a five-year-old son could ring the bell for his mother, putting a note in a son's suitcase to inform the mother he had been sick during his visit, and attending music recitals, sports events, or church services at which their children were present.

Judges issue these orders because there are negative consequences for them if they do not. Federally funded feminist groups publish the names of judges who persist in trying to observe due process. A Maine judge was removed from the bench for "lack of sensitivity" to women applying for restraining orders. One retired judge says his colleagues see the harm being done, but "remain quiet due to the political climate."

Cases have gotten into the news of husbands attacking their estranged wives "despite being under a restraining order." Baskerville asks us to consider whether such men might not be attacking their wives *because* of the restraining orders. These tyrannical acts have much the character of a deliberate provocation. One journalist writes: "It's amazing there aren't more rampages." Of course, to feminists, this "male violence" simply proves the need for more restraining orders: An ideology is unfalsifiable.

There are now "supervised visitation centers" where fathers are made to pay up to $80 an hour to see their children. "People yell at you in front of the children," says one father; "they try to degrade the father in the child's eyes." "Even hugging your own children could end your visit," says another. There are cameras on the walls, and social workers armed with clipboards observe the fathers minutely. The *Boston Globe* reports: "Visitation centers are becoming so popular with family court judges . . . that certain centers . . . have waiting lists up to a year long. That has led to visits being cut short to accommodate other families."

Special "integrated domestic violence courts" are now being established to expedite convictions. "There is no presumption of innocence, hearsay evidence is admissible and defendants have no right to face their accusers. One study found there was no possibility that a defendant could be found innocent, since all persons arrested . . . received some punishment." Prosecutors pile up charges to encourage plea-bargaining; in other words, innocent men plead guilty to lesser charges in an attempt to avoid having their lives entirely ruined.

"Battered women's shelters" are another institution of the divorce industry, no longer bearing any relation to what their name appears to signify. Rather than providing first aid and other physical relief to women brutalized by their husbands, they are "one stop divorce shops." They assist women in fabricating abuse and incest allegations against their husbands and provide "letters of endorsement" for use against fathers in family court. Women report the use of high-pressure tactics to get them to divorce their husbands; one called a shelter "an experience from hell; the message was you believe what we believe, you do what we say, or get out of here." Many shelters are lesbian covens where heterosexual volunteers are forbidden to discuss their wedding plans with coworkers.

The great irony about the entire abuse industry is that child abuse is much *more* likely to occur in the fatherless homes now being created in unprecedented numbers. Sometimes it is perpetrated by the mother's new boyfriends, but very often by the mother herself. HHS studies report that "children in mother-only households were three times more likely to be fatally abused [murdered] than children in father-only households. Females were 78% of the perpetrators of fatal child abuse [murder] and 81% of natural parents who seriously abuse their children." One writer says "although, as a literary theme, the 'good father' protecting his children from the 'bad mother' is almost unheard of (so idealized has mothering become), in real life fathers have often played the protector role inside families." In other words, the abuse industry is depriving children of their natural protectors and fostering more abuse.

Perhaps we may most appropriately conclude this (very incomplete) survey of divorce industry horrors by noting the effects on the children themselves. One study based on interviews with children of divorce reported that they

> expressed the wish for increased contact with their fathers with a startling and moving intensity. . . . The most striking response among six-to-eight-year-old children was their pervasive sadness. The impact of separation appeared so strong that the children's usual defenses and coping strategies did not hold sufficiently under stress. Crying and sobbing were not uncommon. . . . More than half of these children missed their father acutely. Many felt abandoned and rejected by him and expressed their longing in ways reminiscent of grief for a dead parent. . . . In confronting the despair and sadness of these children and their intense, almost physical, longing for the father, it was evident that inner psychological needs of great power and intensity were being expressed.

Inevitably, there has been talk of "reforming" the system — not least by its beneficiaries, who speak of wanting to make it more "efficient." Why we should wish to see children removed from their fathers' care more "efficiently" they do not tell us. The government is fertile with "responsible fatherhood" programs, "healthy marriage" initiatives, "defense of marriage" acts, and suchlike. These should fool no one who has read Dr. Baskerville's book attentively; they are nothing but further occasions for extending governmental power and patronage while deceiving the public. The next time you hear a politician promise to "strengthen" your marriage or family, pay no attention.

What must be done is clear. In the words of columnist Kathleen Parker: "The divorce industry has to be dismantled, burned and buried like the monster it is."

Now we must consider the means for accomplishing this.

One researcher reports being told the same thing in several cities: "Shoot the judges and lawyers!" A few men do more than talk. "Statistics are scarce [why?], but judges and lawyers nationwide agree from all the stories they hear about fatal shootings, bombings, knifings, and beatings that family law is the most dangerous area in which to practice," reports a law journal. According to the *Boston Globe*, judges now carry guns under their robes to protect themselves from fathers. Baskerville asserts that metal detectors were installed in courthouses specifically from fear of fathers. Previous attacks upon family court judges, he notes, went mostly unreported in the press [why?], but the June 2006 shooting of a Nevada judge received international attention. The full gravity of the situation is finally penetrating the public's consciousness. The author pointedly asks "what judges and lawyers expect when they set about the business of taking away people's children."

Indeed, he is neither exaggerating nor using metaphor when, in the book's subtitle, he describes the regime's campaign against fathers as a war. The male obligation to military service—i.e., to die or kill under certain circumstances if called upon—has traditionally been based upon a man's obligation to protect his family; the duty of *national* defense is derived from this, as the nation is itself derived from the family. In the author's words, "this is precisely what fathers are for: to become violent when someone interferes with their children."

Individual acts of revenge, heartwarming though they may be to read about, will not put an end to the system. The liquidation of the divorce regime can only be accomplished by orga-

nized political force. The criminals and parasites who make up
the divorce industry have a big head start; they are highly orga-
nized, well-funded (largely by their victims), determined, and,
in the case of feminists, fanatical. They will fight tooth-and-nail
to retain their wealth and power. Fathers, in contrast, are only
beginning to awaken to the full extent of the situation and to organize resistance. Dr. Baskerville himself is president of one
such organization, the American Coalition for Fathers and Children.

His recommendations for reform are all moderate and sensible — that may be their principal failing. They include the enforcement of due process principles as enshrined in the U.S.
Constitution, a presumption of joint custody, the reform of "no
fault" laws to require faithless women (or men) to take responsibility for ending the marriage contract, and holding divorce industry officials accountable for their decisions.

I am unsure why divorce could not simply be abolished as a
legal category. There do have to be laws to deal with cases of
spousal infidelity and abandonment, of course. Columnist Lloyd
Conway has formulated a simple policy for these, which I am
unable to improve upon: "If you want to run off with a chorus
girl, go ahead — just leave your wallet with Momma. And if the
milkman is making special deliveries, then the lovebirds can fill
out your child support checks together." Holding divorce officials responsible for their decisions will be unnecessary when
they are made responsible for punching out license plates instead. Legal custody will have less practical importance in the
absence of a divorce enforcement regime.

Men, I fear, will have to demand nothing less than the full
reestablishment of what feminists call patriarchy — the male-
headed family as the normal social unit. This may be a "radical"
idea, given how far our society has gone off-track, but it is hardly revolutionary. It is really just the radical restoration of the
natural and traditional order of the human family. Baskerville
doubts whether a return to father custody can "find acceptance
beyond the fringe of political debate." I think he is mistaken
about this. There is no such thing as a fixed "fringe" to political
debate. One of the most important forms of political activity

consists precisely in moving the fringe. It took much more determination on the part of homosexuals to get us to where "gay marriage" is discussed with a straight face than it would for normal men to restore the presumption of father custody. Indeed, I suspect that men, once politically united, could dictate almost any terms they wished to women.

There are interesting times ahead for men. The course we must embark on is dangerous, but it is less dangerous than continuing to do nothing.

The Occidental Quarterly, vol. 7, no. 2 (Summer 2007): 1–23

THE FEMININE SEXUAL COUNTER-REVOLUTION & ITS LIMITATIONS

Wendy Shalit
Girls Gone Mild: Young Women Reclaim Self-Respect and Find It's Not Bad to Be Good
New York: Random House, 2007

Wendy Shalit is back. She first came to public attention in 1995 with a hilarious article in *Commentary* magazine about the rise and fall of co-ed bathrooms at Williams College ("A Ladies' Room of One's Own," August 1995). Freshmen of both sexes were to share a dorm, and determined by consensus that separate men's and women's lavatories would be unnecessary. In fact, all the girls would have preferred separate facilities, but none wanted to admit it for fear of being thought prudish. One developed urinary-tract problems from her reluctance to make use of the co-ed restroom until a point of extreme urgency had been reached. Further investigation revealed that the men were not altogether pleased with the arrangement either. A kind of "Emperor's new clothes" situation had arisen in which a group was imposing something on its members that few or none of them actually wanted.

Shalit came to understand that the sexual revolution as a whole had a similar character: young people were "hooking up" not because they personally desired to but because they believed it was expected of them. The campus feminists pushing casual sex at Williams seemed deeply unhappy. Elsewhere, she met Orthodox Jewish girls—forbidden even to touch their fiancés before the wedding—doing just fine. Braving the shaming tactics of peers and some professors, she wrote a senior thesis on modesty. The project eventually became the book *A Return to Modesty: Rediscovering the Lost Virtue* (New York: The Free Press, 1997), an investigation into the nature of modesty, drawing on the Bible, Rousseau, Kierkegaard, Jean-Paul Sartre's girlfriend, works of visual art, popular records, and *Mademoiselle* magazine.

A Return to Modesty was greeted with outrage from predictable quarters, such as pornographers and feminists. Baby-boomer reviewers accused her of "trying to turn back the clock," the *New York Observer* printed a front-page caricature of her dressed as an SS officer, and she received death threats (p. 5). Her nonchalance about this sort of criticism is fittingly expressed by the inclusion in this new book of her personal *apple pie recipe*: a pie in the face of her "bad girl" critics, so to speak (p. 263). Her self-assurance has no doubt been reinforced by the thousands of grateful letters and e-mails she has received from young women.

The most interesting personal experience she relates involved an invitation, following on the success of her first book, to appear on a PBS program called "If Women Ruled the World." While preparing to interview her, "the producer began to explain what he wanted me to say: that a certain second wave feminist had saved womankind and that I, as a young woman, was grateful to her." When she expressed reservations about the woman's ideas, "the producer began to get impatient: 'What you're saying,' he sputtered, 'isn't in the script!'" (p. 19). In the end, she was not interviewed. She came to enjoy the ludicrousness of a male television producer doing a "powerful women" documentary and telling his female interviewees exactly what to say.

Her new offering, *Girls Gone Mild*, is less ambitious than her earlier book, omitting philosophical speculation on the deeper nature of modesty in favor of reportage on social and sexual trends among young women. The work draws on "over 100 in-depth interviews with girls and young women ages twelve to twenty-eight; fifteen interviews with young men; and over 3,000 e-mail exchanges" as well as a fair amount of travel and discussion with professionals of various sorts.

She begins by describing the popular Bratz dolls, with high-heels and lipsticky come-hither looks, now marketed to girls age 7 to 12. A glossy magazine designed to accompany the dolls asks its young readers to ponder such weighty questions as "Are you always the first in your group to wear the hottest new looks?" and "Do you love it when people look at you in the street?" (p. xvii). For their younger sisters, there is already a Bratz Babyz series—baby dolls with fishnet stockings and miniskirts (p. xv). Such merchandise influences girls' behavior, of course. One reader wrote to Shalit of

> two little girls who live on our street who are maybe five and seven who dress in platform shoes, miniskirts, belly shirts, etc. One day they saw some boys playing baseball on the field near our house and got all dressed up with makeup, purses, etc. to walk down there and show off (p. xix)

There is now even a word for such children: prostitots (Shalit does not mention the circumstance, highly suspicious to this reviewer, that widespread hysteria over "pedophiles" has developed simultaneously.)

On the other hand, she reports on girls who have staged successful boycotts (called "girlcotts") of companies pushing immodest clothing (pp. 224-31). This countercurrent appears to be gathering strength: The rate of virginity among teenagers has risen for ten straight years (p. 75).

This male reviewer's eyelids got heavy, however, when the author went into the details of staging an amateur "modest fashion show" (pp. 170-72). While no doubt preferable to having girls modeling thongs or Frederick's of Hollywood negligees, we might better advise them to limit the time and money they spend on personal adornment altogether. How about substituting an event where we dress the girls in barrels with shoulder straps and teach them the uses of various household cleaning agents?

Adolescents who have outgrown their Bratz dolls can move on to *Gossip Girl*, a popular series of novels that Shalit describes as "the Marquis de Sade for teens." Readers are led to fantasize about having modeling contracts, closets bulging with designer fashions, drawers stuffed with diamond accessories, and complicated love-lives involving a "best friend's boyfriend." One female character is described as "not afraid to play dirty to get what she wants" (pp. 181-82). Girls unable to invest the effort required to read the books now have the option of watching the television series.

By way of contrast, the author introduces the reader to "L.T. Meade," or Elizabeth Thomasina Meade Smith (1854-1914), American author of 280 books for girls, including such racy titles as *A Very Naughty Girl*, *The Rebel of the School*, and *Wild Kitty*. These books were churned out with about the same speed as the Gossip Girl novels, but they all contained a moral message. By the end of each novel, writes Shalit, a "character defect was expunged, but the girl's spirit remained in full force." The reform often involves the heroine's learning to consider the needs of others hurt by her previous self-centered behavior. Modest as Meade's artistic aims were, her characters *are* distinct: each "naughty" girl is naughty in a slightly different way. The Gossip Girls are more or less interchangeable ciphers compounded of greed, lust, and cunning (pp. 184-86). Home-schoolers take note: you may want to consider passing over Barnes & Noble in favor of an antiquarian shop.

Many of Shalit's anecdotes involve the strange new "generation gap" between baby-boomer parents and their offspring. Those old enough to remember when "the establishment" was a fighting term will be amused to read of rebellious teenage girls who declare "we're the establishment, because nobody else wants to establish things" (p. 60).

The boomers thought—and still think—that courtship rituals and marital fidelity were mere shackles upon healthy desire. So they encourage their own children to do as they please. But the old rules were less shackles than guideposts; the young feel not liberated but lost without them. In other words, being told to "do whatever you want!" is unhelpful to adolescents still trying to figure out what they want. Often, their parents' well-meaning encouragement is experienced by them as pressure to engage in sexual behavior they do not truly desire. Girls report having sex with strangers simply in order to "fit in." One teenage boy sobs, "I don't think my mom loves me," because she does nothing to prevent his sleeping with an older woman (p. 8).

Commendably, the author devotes space to aspects of popular culture many writers (and possibly some of my readers) deem beneath their notice, such as *Cosmopolitan* magazine. She asks rhetorically:

> Does it even matter what the women's magazines say? "Serious writers" often tell me that "we all know" women's magazines are not to be taken seriously.
>
> I beg to differ. The intelligentsia's dismissal of *Cosmo* masquerades as sophistication but could hardly be more clueless. Perhaps it is necessary to state the obvious: The reason these magazines are available in every supermarket everywhere is that tens of millions of women are buying and reading them. (pp. 82-83)

Indeed, *Cosmopolitan* is the top-selling magazine in American college bookstores. It is not too much to call it an important part of an American woman's education. When the author mentioned to a young, religiously observant woman that some people do not think *Cosmo* should be taken seriously, she "was shocked and drew in her breath sharply: 'Are you kidding me? *Cosmo*? It's, like, the Bible!'"

An editor at *Seventeen* magazine told her:

> Honestly, I didn't think much of teen mags before working with one, but I know that girls take *Seventeen* very seriously. Sometimes it scared me to learn just how much girls really looked to the magazine for advice. You wouldn't believe the kinds of questions they would ask — things they should have been asking their parents but couldn't or wouldn't. (p. 83)

In other words, these cheap, mass-produced publications command tremendous moral authority with their readership: how well are we to suppose the selection process for editors ensures their ability to measure up to the responsibility?

Women's magazines, in contrast to those marketed to men, contain almost nothing but advice. Men do seek advice, of course, but usually in particular and limited areas where they already have their goal in view. Women are comparatively rudderless. "The one thing I heard over and over" from interviewees, Shalit says, "was how desperate they were for a new set of role models" (p. xi). So much for the independent women feminism promised us.

Indeed, if our natural perceptions were not distorted by 40 years of feminist cant about "women leaders," it would be perfectly obvious that most women feel a strong need for guidance, and this is one reason marriage is so important for their happiness. Their rage and frustration with men today is partly owing to men's failure to provide them with the loving but firm leadership they require.

Shalit devotes one chapter to profiling young women who are actively speaking out in favor of premarital chastity. It is remarkable that most of them are black. The author notes that black colleges such as Spellman have stricter parietals than elite, mostly white Northeastern institutions such as the one she herself attended, and that "all the writers who have attacked me, calling modesty an 'elite white' concept, are in fact elite white people" (p. 66). She even slips in some boilerplate about "offensive racist stereotypes" and "the painful legacy of slavery." My readers are possibly aware that such "stereotypes" have a real biological basis: Africans are in fact less monogamous than Europeans. But the author is merely reporting what she sees when she writes about the prominence of black women in the modesty movement. What could account for it?

Shalit acknowledges that the taboo on honest discussion of race makes this a difficult topic to approach. She found just one sociologist willing to address it, under condition of anonymity. He told her simply: "Black women have paid the heaviest price from the sexual revolution in the United States" (p. 72).

Here is my conjecture. It is an old observation that sexual morality is most strict among people of moderate means; looser behavior occurs among the very rich (because they can afford it) and the very poor (because they do not calculate the consequences). The worst possible situation arises when the poor become artificially "rich," by their own standards, through welfare payments. Now, the elite white brats who pioneered the sexual revolution on campuses in the '60s were able to draw upon the capital laboriously built up by parents toughened in depression and war. Low-intelligence underclass blacks, at the opposite extreme, get their babies subsidized by taxpayers; they are actually rewarded for not having a male breadwinner. You will find even less sexual fidelity among them than among white college kids or the Hollywood glitterati. Shalit, however, did not plumb the social depths of the housing projects. The black women she talked with are managing to keep their head above water, and this group, unsubsidized and in moderate circumstances, has the most to fear from male abandonment. Economic deterioration may eventually present many white women with a similar set of incentives. The criminal behavior of "Family Courts" in systematically rewarding female abandonment is delaying this development, however.

One of the many reasons for limiting sexual relations to marriage is that it reduces competition between persons of the same sex, making friendship and trust possible between them. Shalit devotes a chapter to this subject. In a traditional religious community in Israel, she watched women drop what they were doing and dance until they teared up with happiness whenever they learned that one of them was to be married. "The idea of women being truly happy for one another, without any reservations, was new to me and also very moving," she writes (p. 134).

In America, by contrast, popular girls' T-shirts carry messages such as "Do I Make You Look Fat?" and "Blondes are Adored . . . Brunettes are Ignored." Among the motives behind the recent successful "girlcotting" of stores selling such shirts, in fact, is girls' awareness that they encourage cliques and bullying among themselves (p. 225).

Reportedly, an increasing number of American girls are choosing to socialize only with boys because, as one such girl's mother explains, "teen girls are often brutally manipulative and mean" (p. 128). Experts report that "girls are committing significantly more acts of violence than they did even one generation ago" (p. 243). The author relates disturbing stories of girls actually driven to suicide by the bullying of their "friends" (pp. 254-55).

Girls may be behaving so badly in part because it is what they are now being taught. The author tells of one mother who

was "determined to raise a feminist." By the time her little girl
was 2, the nursery school was complaining of her bullying the 5-
year-olds (she would jump up in order to hit them). The mother
says, "I encouraged her to 'go for it.'" Another female lawyer
told her, "I am very suspicious of telling girls they need to be
morally good. That's sexism right there" (p. 251). Shalit quotes
articles from the popular feminist magazine *Bitch* ridiculing self-
less and considerate women and unfavorably contrasting them
with others who show a "dark side" (p. 241). A certain Elizabeth
Wurtzel has written a whole book titled *Bitch* in which she declares: "For a woman to do just as she pleases and dispense with
other people's needs, wants, demands, and desires continues to
be revolutionary" (p. 242).

A highly successful women's magazine editor has written a
book of advice for young wives stating: "Giving, devoting, sacri-
ficing . . . these are the actions of a good wife, no? No. These are
the actions of a drudge, a sucker, a sap." Instead, women are
urged to emulate a wife who threw her husband's clothes into
the garden to teach him not to leave socks on the floor: "He understood I meant it." Or another who wanted her husband to
help with the laundry, and hollered at him: "Are you a f***ing
retard that you don't see me running up and down stairs? Listen
to me and stop your bulls**t." Or another who discovered this
interpersonal skill: "Just stand there and start screaming. If you
stand there and scream long enough, someone is going to realize
that you're standing in the middle of the room screaming [and
ask] 'Why are you screaming?'" (pp. 245-47).

What could be wrong with men these days that they refuse to
commit?

It is remarkable that a woman with such traditional ideas
about marriage, modesty, and feminine decorum never con-
demns feminism per se. Instead, Shalit claims to have perceived
a "fourth wave" of the movement characterized by the rejection
of pornography and casual sex. This reviewer is not sanguine
about the possibility of an eventual Nth feminist wave coming
along to solve all the problems created by waves 1 through (N –
1). Shalit does better when she acknowledges that feminism has
"become a sort of Rohrschach test: the word itself has become

almost meaningless—and can refer to diametrically opposed ideas" (p. 208). The young self-described feminists she quotes do sound extremely confused. They say things such as "I don't think the first feminists wanted us to be more like men" (p. 218) and "Feminism has always been about valuing home life" (p. 222). Some are simply using "feminist" to mean feminine (p. 121).

My impression, however, is that a couple things have in fact persisted through all these waves and permutations: an emphasis on "empowerment" for women, and the presumption that men are to blame for most of their problems. In at least this minimal sense, Wendy Shalit might be called a feminist.

* * *

The present reviewer is entirely in sympathy with a return to feminine modesty and the limiting of sexual relations to marriage. But this allows plenty of room for disagreement as to how our society got so far off track and the best means of returning to normal, healthy courtship and monogamy. In particular, the notion that all our problems come from women's making sex available outside marriage—and, consequently, that a "holding out for the wedding" strategy will make everything right again—deserves a close, critical look. Wendy Shalit's writings provide a useful occasion for doing this. Her proposals have considerable limitations, in fact, most of which flow from a single source: feminine narcissism and its concomitant unconcern for the masculine point of view.

I wish to be fair, so I will point out that her first book, *A Return to Modesty* (hereafter abbreviated RM), contained glimmers of such a concern. Sexual harassment law, she complained, "treats men like dogs. It says to them, *Down, boy, down!* Don't do X, because I say so" (RM, p. 102). She insightfully noted that women can elicit desirable male behavior through moral authority far more effectively than they could ever impose it through the police power of the state. This is far removed from the usual feminist mentality.

In her new book *Girls Gone Mild* (hereafter GGM), however,

the male viewpoint is almost totally disregarded (She acknowledges the neglect but offers poor reasons for it: GGM, p. 277.) She even describes her indignation at a woman who reminded her, after a long discussion of girls and their problems, that, after all, the boys have feelings too: "I was speechless. Emotional, dreamy girls are a thorn in our side, but when boys are romantic, their every tear is precious" (GGM, p. 90).

My point is not that we should coddle boys; I am simply calling attention to the difficulty Shalit, in common with most women, seems to have with putting herself imaginatively in the place of a male. There may well be an evolutionary explanation for this. Men instinctively protect women because the future of the tribe lies in the children they bear. Women have adapted to this state of affairs, and it colors their moral outlook. They do not spend much time worrying about the well-being of men. Even getting them to cook supper for their husbands is probably a triumph of civilization. Their natural inclination is to let men look after themselves and take their chances in life. At the same time, they count on men to shield *them* from the harsher aspects of reality, and become extremely indignant at any men who fail to do so. In other words, women are naturally inclined to assume that men must take responsibility for everyone, while they are only responsible for themselves and the children. Young, still-childless women have no one left to think about but themselves and easily fall into self-absorption. One popular women's magazine is actually titled *Self*. I would not want the job of promoting a magazine of that title to men.

One aspect of female narcissism is a failure to think in terms of moral reciprocity. For example, here is a male columnist (Fred Reed) praising the intolerance of Mexican women for infidelity: "They can also be savagely jealous, to the point of removing body parts. But for this I respect them. Any woman worth having has every right to expect her man to keep his pants up except in her presence. He owes to her what she owes to him. Fair is fair." This is the way a man thinks. A woman is more likely to think, "I get to do as I please and you get to do as I please: fair is fair."

Does the reader suspect me of indulging in a cheap shot here?

Consider, first, this passage from Shalit's first book: "Many etiquette books, in both England and America, stressed a woman's prerogative to greet a man on the street first, particularly if he was not a close friend. If she chose to greet him, he was obligated to respond in kind, but if she passed him by, there was absolutely nothing he could do about it" (RM, p. 56).

I do not mean to take issue with this rule of etiquette, which may well have a sensible rationale. My point is simply that its one-sidedness does not seem problematic or in need of explanation to Shalit. A man might at least ask whether there is some larger context that explains why, in this particular case, all rights should be with the woman and none with the man.

Second, let us consider the more important matter of sexual intimacy. Shalit is, of course, emphatic on a man's lack of all sexual rights before the wedding. Referring to a girl whose boyfriend began "pressuring" her for sex after *eight months* of courtship, her assessment is: "If he's pressuring you for sex, he probably doesn't love you" (GGM, p. 29). Now, courtship is typically an interaction in which the man seeks sexual surrender from the woman, and the woman seeks assurance of commitment from the man. Would the author sympathize with a man who reasoned: "If a woman is pressuring me for commitment, she probably doesn't love me"? It does not sound like it: elsewhere, she approvingly quotes a woman who is "mortified" that when girls "hint to their boyfriends about marriage [they] find themselves dumped like garbage" (RM, p. 227). She even refers to the authority of another of her old etiquette books to show that "a young woman could assume that a man wanted to marry her if he simply spent a good chunk of time with her" (GGM, p. 28). (I'm guessing eight months would count as "a good chunk of time.") In other words, women have the right to expect commitment from men, but men are bad when they seek sexual surrender from women; women's instincts are morally valid, but men's are not. (Moreover, Shalit never says a word about the legitimate male fear of divorce, which may well be why the young man in her anecdote was "pressuring" his girlfriend about sex rather than simply proposing marriage.)

An old-fashioned fellow might agree with the author's disapproval of premarital sex, but probably on the assumption that she would at least acknowledge the husband's claims after the ceremony. This assumption would be mistaken, however. Once the couple is married, the wife's sexual desires and the *duty* of the husband to satisfy them become her exclusive concern (RM, pp. 114-15). When she comes across a case of a couple where the man was the party less eager for physical intimacy, her sympathy is once again with the woman; she asks: "If he has no interest in a mutually satisfying relationship, why not just leave?" (GGM, p. 177).

I believe Shalit is by no means unusually narcissistic, as women go. Most do take for granted men's obligation to put women's needs and desires before their own, and thus to feel no particular gratitude when men do so. Many women have no idea, for example, how intense a young man's sexual urges can be, and are not inclined to treat this powerful force of nature with the necessary respect. Shalit never seems aware that men feel "pressured" by their *own* sexual urges, or that a normal, healthy young man who has dated a girl for eight months before making these urges known has already demonstrated a fair amount of self-control.

Lack of a sense of moral reciprocity and of an ability to empathize with men leads many women, in fact, into a kind of schizophrenic attitude toward male desire. Most of the time they complain about how annoying it is and seem to wish it would go away entirely. But they do, of course, want some man to marry them. In other words, men's sexual desires are supposed to be weak enough never to inconvenience women, but at the same time strong enough that they gladly exchange all their independence and most of their income whenever some woman does, after all, decide to take a mate. The *desideratum* would appear to be a man whose natural urges are like a faucet that women could turn on and off at their own convenience.

It is true that actual men fall short of this "dildo ideal," as it might be called. No restoration of feminine modesty is going to change the situation, however, or eliminate the need for women to compromise with men. Children who insist on having everything their own way eventually learn that no one wants to play with them anymore; women who follow Wendy Shalit's advice of "waiting and keeping their standards high" may find that the wait lasts all the way to menopause.

When the sexual revolution began, women imagined that the "slavery" of marriage was unfairly standing between themselves and endless erotic fulfillment. Forty years later, many are imagining instead that the availability to men of sex outside marriage is standing in the way of their wedding. "If other women were not sluts," they reason, "the man of my dreams would be forced to discover my true value and come crawling to me with a diamond ring." One of the interviewees from Shalit's first book, for example, complains: "After three dates when I wouldn't sleep with [a certain man], he dumped me, just like that! If you ask me, it's because it's way too easy for them. Why should they waste time with a girl like me when they can get it for free?" (RM, p. 104).

Now, how does the woman know this is the reason he "dumped" (stopped courting) her? Never once have I heard a woman say: "I am such a pain in the derriere that after just three dates men are charging for the exit." Appealing to the supposed universal availability of sex has become a way for women to avoid facing the reality of rejection. Men break off courtships for all kinds of reasons: they may sense that a particular girl might not be faithful, is not careful with money, has too many bad habits, or just plain is not for them. Holding out for wedding rings is not going to solve these women's problems and allow them to live happily ever after. If we could wave a magic wand and cause extramarital sex to disappear overnight, many women would be shocked to discover that handsome movie stars were still not flocking to their doorsteps with flowers and chocolates.

Indeed, I have heard men remark on the oddity that sex seems to be the only card women have to play in the dating game any more. They do not know how to manage a household, raise children, or treat a husband. Instead, like prostitutes, they think entirely in terms of maximizing the return they get on sex. Even Shalit acknowledges an inability to cook at the time of her marriage. (That apple pie recipe of hers begins, "You will need two frozen premade pie crusts . . .") A renewed focus on feminine modesty, while welcome, will not by itself prepare young women for their domestic duties. The attitude that "I'm too good to sleep around" in the absence of anything to offer men besides sex may result not in any epidemic of marriage proposals but in widespread spinsterhood enlivened only by occasional readings of *The Vagina Monologues*, the lesbian-feminist play in which women gush over how wonderful their own private parts are.

But let us consider Shalit's own account, culled from anecdotes and women's magazines, of the sexual situation women face today. The humble corporate drone who has to fear harassment charges and loss of livelihood if he winks at the girl in the next cubicle will feel as if he stepped through Alice's looking glass when he reads this material. Here is a realm in which men have reduced women to struggling to see who can offer them the most and the best sex, frantically searching the Kama Sutra for some new position or technique that will manage to gratify their cloyed appetites. The men who inhabit this world are concerned not that women remain faithful, but that they do not become "clingy." *Cosmo* supports them, advising women to scurry out the door immediately after sex for fear of intruding on the Big Important things their man has to do that day that do not involve them—and that may well include a tryst with another girlfriend. "It's sad to see that this is what it's come to," says one woman: "that guys will raise the bar and girls will scramble to meet it. Women just want to know what they have to do to get these guys to fall in love with them" (GGM, p. 176). One young woman explains: "If I don't do whatever [my boyfriend] wants and he broke up with me for some reason, two days from now he'd have somebody else. That's just how it works" (GGM, p. 177). "The men who share these women's beds," says Shalit, "are treated like kings or princes whose authority comes from God himself, whereas the women's own feelings and even their health concerns are restricted in the extreme" (GGM, p. 81). Shalit advises one such woman to "run, not walk, to the nearest exit, trying not to trip over all the naked women on her way out" (GGM, p. 79).

All these stories certainly make it appear that, in the brave new world of the sexual revolution, the man's position is stronger than under monogamy while the woman's is weaker. In fact, nothing could be farther from the truth. Let me pose a simple question that Shalit never considers. It used to be that there was roughly one girl for every boy; if men now have harems, *where are the extra women coming from?*

The answer is equally simple and obvious. Most men do not have harems, of course, and there are no more women than formerly. Some men have harems because women "liberated" from monogamy mate only with unusually attractive men. This situation demonstrates not the weakness of the woman's position but its strength. If the male sex instinct were the primary determinant of mating, the overall pattern would be the most attractive women getting gang-banged.

In order to understand what is really going on, it will be necessary to shine a harsh light on a matter women instinctively prefer to keep under wraps: the female sex drive. Shalit almost never refers to it, and there is even a certain appropriateness about this, since such reticence is part of the feminine modesty she is trying to reestablish. But it means a veil is drawn over some important circumstances that must be honestly confronted if marriage and the natural family are to be restored as social norms.

When a young girl becomes erotically aware of boys, she is endowed by nature with a set of blinders that exclude the majority of them—including many who can make good husbands—from her sight. What gets a male within her narrow range of vision is called "sexual attractiveness." What is it?

It is not possible to find out by asking women themselves. They will insist until they are blue in the face that they want only a sensitive, respectful fellow who treats them right. "Intelligence, kindness, personality [and] a certain sense of humor" make up Wendy Shalit's list of supposedly sought-after male qualities (RM, p. 116). In a passage on the decline of male courtesy she delivers the following ludicrous assertion deadpan: "When . . . a man does dare to open a door for a woman, he is snapped up right away" (RM, p. 156).

When women claim to be seeking kindness, respect, a sense

of humor, etc., they mean at most that they would like to find these qualities in the men who are already within their erotic field of view. When a man asks what women are looking for, he is trying to find out how he can get into that field of view. Women do not normally say, either because they do not know themselves or because it embarrasses them to speak about it. The advice they do give harms a lot of lonely men who mistakenly concentrate their mating effort on showing kindness and courtesy to ungrateful brats rather than working to gain the things females actually respond to.

Fortunately, we do not have to depend upon female testimony. It is with women as with politicians: if you wish to understand them you must ignore what they say and watch what they do. Plentiful evidence gathered over a vast range of history and culture leaves no room for doubt: women are attracted to men who possess some combination of physical appearance, social status, and resources.

In the environment in which we evolved, the careful choice of a mate was critical to a female's success in passing on her genes. If her man was not strong enough to be a successful hunter, or not of sufficiently high rank within the tribe to commandeer food from others, her children might be in trouble. The women who were reproductively successful were those with a sexual preference for effective providers. A kind of erotic "tunnel vision" was selected for, which causes women to focus their mating effort on the men at the top of the pack—the "alpha males" with good physical endowments, social rank, and economic resources (or an ability to acquire them). Today the female preference for tall men, to give just one example, no longer makes much sense, but they, and we, are stuck with it.

What women instinctively want is for 99 percent of the men they run into to leave them alone, buzz off, drop dead—while the one to whom they feel attracted makes all their dreams come true. One of the keys to deciphering female speech is that the term "men" signifies for them only the very restricted number of men they find sexually attractive. All the dirty articles in *Cosmo* about "giving him the sex he craves" and "driving him wild in bed" concern this man of her dreams, who by some amazing coincidence usually turns out to be the man of some other girl's dreams as well.

During their nubile years, many women are at least as concerned with turning male desire off (i.e., telling the 99 percent to drop dead) as with turning it on (getting Mr. Alpha to commit): they get more offers of attention than they have time to process. Cunning feminists, many of them lesbians, have exploited this circumstance to the hilt, convincing naive young women they are being "harassed." Quietly observing the furor over so-called harassment during the past two decades, I wondered how these women could fail to realize that the men of whom they were complaining constituted their pool of potential husbands and that they could not afford to alienate all of them. Clearly, I overestimated their intelligence. And Wendy Shalit does not distinguish herself in this respect either; she uses the term "harassment" as freely and uncritically as any man-hating feminist could wish.

But surely North America's leading spokesman for feminine modesty would never encourage young women to date simply on the basis of their sexual urges?

Well, let's see. At one point in her first book she is discussing a woman's use of the controversial drug Prozac to help her "date calmly." She then blurts out: "Maybe a woman shouldn't be dating calmly—maybe it should be dizzying and tailspinning and all the rest. Maybe the floor should drop" (RM, p. 165). What she is describing here is female sexual arousal; it takes an emotional form. Her statement is the precise female equivalent of a man saying: "Men shouldn't date calmly—they should date only young hotties with fantastic legs, hourglass figures, etc." What would Wendy Shalit think of that advice?

Now, let me be clear: I do not have any objection *per se* to every woman being able to marry a stunningly handsome, successful man who makes her swoon in blissful passion eternally, yadda, yadda; I am merely pointing out that the world does not work this way, and men are not to blame that it doesn't.

Moreover, there is nothing in the definition of marriage about the man (or woman) being attractive. That is because the marriage vow lays out the duties of the two spouses. Duty implies possibility. A man usually can, with considerable self-control and sacrifice, remain faithful to a single woman and support her and the children; he cannot become a romance novel hero and turn his wife's life into a perpetual honeymoon.

The traditional answer to the question, "How do I get Mr. Tall-Dark-and-Handsome to commit?" is, "You probably won't." Those men go fast, and they usually go to the most attractive females. But that does not, of course, guarantee the contentment of those females either: four women walked out on Cary Grant. Part of the folk wisdom of all ages and peoples has been that sexual attraction is an inadequate basis for matrimony.

Monogamy means that women are not permitted to mate with a man, however attractive, once he has been claimed by another woman. It does not get a more attractive mate for a woman than she would otherwise get; it normally gets her a less attractive one. "Liberated," hypergamous female mating—i.e., what we have now—is what ensures highly attractive mates for most women. But, of course, those mates "don't commit"—really, are unable to commit to all the women who desire them. The average woman must decide between having the most attractive "sex partner" possible and having a permanent husband. If she were serious about seeking commitment, in fact, the rational procedure would be to seek out a particularly unattractive man, i.e., one for whom there is the least possible competition. This thought seldom occurs to young women, however.

For an ordinary man to mate with a woman, either (1) he must work himself into her field of erotic vision (e.g., by amassing wealth and achieving status—*not* by demonstrating that he is "kind" and "respectful of women"); or (2) she must take off the blinders and widen her own field of vision until it includes him. This latter is what I term the "grandmother effect." Young women used to be routinely advised by their elders not to base their behavior toward men upon sexual attraction, despising ordinary men and immodestly throwing themselves at good-looking, high-status men. Most young women concluded from this that grandma was just too old to understand love. But sometimes the advice may actually have had a slight effect. Consider the words to a popular song from 1963:

I always dreamed the boy I loved would come along
And he'd be tall and handsome, rich and strong.
Now that boy I love has come to me,
But he sure ain't the way I thought he'd be.
He doesn't look like a movie star,
He doesn't drive a Cadillac car,
He sure ain't the boy I've been dreaming of,
But he's sure the boy I love.

(By the time the song is over, we learn the boyfriend is living off unemployment checks.)

Shalit is no grandma. Besides telling young women that dating is supposed to be tailspinning, she frequently urges them to maintain "high standards" and speaks with fond nostalgia of the days when a suitor was required to "prove his worthiness" to a woman. This sounds delightful, no doubt, but the effect depends on weasel terms. Romantic young men will want to conceive of the "worthiness" they must demonstrate as a moral quality—as being a gentleman, in fact. Young women are more likely to interpret it to mean that they "deserve" a romance-novel hero. To them, "maintaining high standards" will suggest that they should keep their erotic blinders at the narrowest possible setting.

This is not modesty but delusion. The reason men found wives before the sexual revolution was not that they were "worthier" than the date-raping sex-maniacs of today (as many male conservative commentators imply), but because women did not have their expectations formed and their imaginations corrupted by the likes of *Cosmo* and *Gossip Girl*. Popular culture's message of limitless gratification has got ignorant girls so worked up over sex that Casanova himself would not be able to satisfy them. Our author's vague talk of "worthiness" and "high standards" does nothing to counteract this tendency, and may reinforce it.

In this book as in her last one, Shalit offers no thoughts about what is to be done with the majority of men who are less than tailspinningly attractive. This, however, is a critical question for any society. It is not simply a matter of hurt feelings. Frankly, no one has ever cared very much about the feelings of such men, as they themselves learn early and well. The reason their sexual situation is a legitimate matter for public concern is that "the devil makes work for idle hands." Poor, low-status bachelors are the most vice-, crime-, and violence-prone group in societies everywhere. No one has ever discovered a better way of employing their time and energies than by making fathers of them. Doing so will, however, involve the immeasurable calamity that certain women will just have to date calmly.

The women the author describes as struggling to get their "sex partners" to commit would be surprised to learn that the indifference of these men to their needs and feelings is precisely paralleled by their own indifference to the majority of men, who remain outside their field of vision. The chief point of distinction, in fact, is that the women's unhappiness is largely the result of their own poor judgment and behavior; the men's often is not.

Shalit, however, speaks as if a man's failure to find a wife were always his own fault. Thus, she writes in an extremely critical vein of men who use pornography as "regressing to infantile sexuality" and "incapable of sustaining an adult sexual relation with a woman" (RM, p. 53). This is perhaps a reasonable position to take for one who believes men can get wives simply by holding doors open for women. But when women are occupied providing harems to a few highly attractive men, many men will perforce find themselves "incapable of sustaining an adult sexual relation with a woman." It does not follow that there is anything wrong with these men. The fault lies with the women who have abandoned their traditional role of enforcing monogamy. Perhaps one should consider instead whether hypergamous mating and careerist deferral of marriage by young women might not be the principal driving force behind the explosive growth of the pornography industry.

Since the sexual revolution began, plenty of "beta males" have been tearing their hair out trying to discover what on Earth they have to do to make themselves acceptable to the *Cosmo* girl next door. They hear it said that women do not want to be rushed into sex and are looking for a man to commit. So when a woman does not respond favorably to his first advances, Mr. Beta reasons that he has to demonstrate his commitment. He will "prove his worthiness" to the angelic creature by being patient, kind, attentive, and respectful—exactly what women claim to want from men. He then gets slapped with a harassment accusation. If the woman is a co-worker he will probably lose his job. (Many—perhaps most—employers will fire a man without a hearing upon a woman's complaint.) The loss of income, of course, does nothing to improve his success with other women.

This pattern may be repeated for many years until, well into his thirties, he unexpectedly finds himself starting to receive come-hither looks from desperate, frustrated, menopausal shrews cast off by more attractive men (or who have divorced such men). Sadly, many men are so lonely that they try to accommodate such women. Then they find themselves on the receiving end of all the resentment against "men" that has been building up in the women's minds all these years. (Female anger tends to be less focused on the particular person who has caused it.)

There is reason to think such accommodation of women is already becoming less common: ordinary men are understandably growing disgusted with cleaning up other people's messes. They are starting to reason as follows: We cannot keep resentful, *Cosmo*-addled, STD-infected harridans out of our schools, workplaces, or government, but at least we can keep them out of our beds. Let them have the glamorous careers the feminist sisterhood fought so hard to obtain for them. They do not need our paychecks to keep them supplied for a lifetime with pulp romance fiction and magazine articles on "Reversing the Aging Process" or "Seven Kinds of Orgasm and How to Have Them All at Once." Everyone makes choices in life and must accept the consequences; they long ago made theirs.

This male sexual counterrevolution—"revenge of the nerds," you might call it—is likely to end up being more important and effective than Shalit's exclusively feminine strategy of keeping the knickers up until after the wedding. What good will that do when there is not going to be a wedding?

Men do not have to prove their worthiness to anybody. They are the ones who bear the primary costs of marriage. It is a woman's responsibility to prove she is worthy of the privilege of becoming a man's helpmeet and bearing his children. It takes a strict upbringing to form a tiny female savage into such a lady. Today, that form of upbringing is mostly a thing of the past: marriageable women are becoming difficult to find, and the costs of searching for them are getting too high.

A man should never base his self-image on what women think of him in any case, because women's concerns are too materialistic and self-centered. ("He that is married careth for the things that are of the world, how he may please his wife," as St. Paul put it.) The men who have accomplished the greatest things for our civilization have not, by and large, resembled the heroes of women's romance fiction; indeed, they have been disproportionately celibate. Once a man realizes what triggers female attraction, and understands that women's judgments of men are largely rationalizations of this attraction (or its absence), he will not be inclined to overvalue their opinion of him.

I mentioned above that Shalit's writing is strongly marked by feminine narcissism; passivity is a second feminine trait that heavily colors her account of women's experiences.

Men, by and large, are doers. They are expected to go out into the world and accomplish something, to strive for success but accept defeat if they must, and always to be strictly accountable for their actions. Women are different. Consider popular romance fiction, that most feminine of literary genres: its key term is "passion," which implies passivity. A hero simply appears on the scene; the helplessness of the heroine to resist him is strongly emphasized. He sweeps her up in his big, strong arms and carries her off to a realm of endless, blissful feelings. He *does*, while she merely *is*.

Romance fiction is, to put it mildly, inconsistent with the traditional Christian view of marriage, in which a woman freely enters into a covenant and is subsequently held strictly responsible for living in accordance with its terms. The contrast might be expressed thus: the Christian view of womanhood is ethical, while the romance-novel heroine is a merely natural being.

The women in Wendy Shalit's anecdotes are of the latter sort: they never seem to do anything. They are like romance heroines in passively submitting to whatever some man does to them, except that they always seem to end up miserable.

In *A Return to Modesty*, for a first example, the author describes T-shirts designed by the campus feminists at Williams College bearing such charming messages as "I HATE YOU!" and "Don't touch me again!" One of the shirts read, "Why does this keep happening to me? When will this end?" (RM, p. 9). The woman appealing for our attention and sympathy with this message apparently does not perceive herself as an agent at all; bad things (presumably involving men) simply "keep happening" to her.

Or again, Shalit recounts an incautious 1 a.m. visit of hers to a summer camp counselor's bedroom when she was a tender 15: "One evening, I suddenly *found myself* [my emphasis] one floor above the room in which I usually slept. This room, as it happens, was the bedroom of my instructor. I don't recall exactly the circumstances under which I had alighted there . . ." (RM, pp. 184-85). A man might be tempted to point out that it probably involved putting one foot in front of the other. I do not wish to be too rough on a girl of 15, but when thousands of adult women complain about "finding themselves" in bed with men who have no interest in marrying them, it is harder to be indulgent.

The problem with a passive mindset is that it involves an abdication of personal responsibility. Shalit wants our sympathy for the way her female interviewees are treated by their boyfriends, but she carefully avoids mentioning how the men got to be their boyfriends. In every case, it happened because the women chose them. The rule of nature is that males display while females choose.

Now let us consider in some detail one of Shalit's unhappy-woman anecdotes which seems to me particularly instructive:

A friend of mine had an affair with her professor when she was 21. She was in his class at the time and madly in love with him; he had no intention of doing anything other than using and summarily disposing of her. I was struck, not that what had *happened to her* [my emphasis] had deeply upset her, but that she felt she had to *apologize*: "this is going to sound really cheesy but, um . . . I mean, for God's sake, he took my virginity!" (RM, p. 11)

Much as I hate to spoil the effect of the touching melodrama the author conjures up for us here, I believe some comments and questions are in order. First, loss of virginity is not something that simply "happens to" a woman. Both author and interviewee speak as if the man "took" his student's virginity like a pickpocket depriving an unwitting victim of a wallet. How exactly was this young lady's attention occupied while the unspeakable defilement of her innocence was taking place?

Second, precisely what is meant by the assertion that the young woman was "madly in love"? Love may be the ultimate weasel term, so for purposes of clarification, let me oppose to the author's anecdote a short one of my own.

I had occasion recently to make some visits to a nursing home. Most of the residents never receive visitors; they just sit, bound to wheelchairs, waiting for death. Such care as they get is provided by low-wage workers speaking Swahili, Amharic, and a Babel of other tongues. Heaven knows where their children or grandchildren are. But a few cases, I noticed, are different. A man who once navigated bombers past Hitler's Luftwaffe was there, unable to feed himself. Every day his wife appeared and sat by him, patiently spooning the food into his mouth. Was he an "alpha male"? Did he make her swoon with passion? Did he support her any longer? Did he, for that matter, provide her with any benefit at all? No: yet she continued to appear every day for months on end, never complaining, until the day he died. This behavior cannot be explained in terms of rational self-interest, and I submit that it might reasonably be called "love."

But love in this sense cannot be demonstrated to exist in a young woman—not even a newly married one; it requires a lifetime to reveal itself. So no one is in a position to say for sure whether Shalit's "madly in love" friend was really prepared to stand by the professor "for richer or for poorer, in sickness and in health," etc.—not even the young woman herself. Even if he had married her *en forme*, there is a good statistical chance she would have ended up divorcing him after a few years (blaming him, as unfaithful wives invariably do, for the "breakdown" of the marriage). We simply cannot know.

When the author describes this woman as "madly in love," however, she is not referring to any active service or sacrifice, but to an emotion. This type of love, especially characteristic of the young, might better be termed infatuation. It is a natural occurrence which always wears off over time. It does not merit the respect we pay to a lifetime of proven marital loyalty.

Shalit's friend probably experienced the podium effect. When a man is addressing an audience, it conveys subrationally to the female mind that he has status: he speaks, while others merely listen. The phenomenon has long been known to Hollywood scriptwriters. Many old Cary Grant romantic comedies contain a scene where the heroine watches him addressing an audience. Shalit could probably tell us plenty about the podium effect herself, if she cared to; she mentions "my admiration for my [future] husband after hearing him speak at a Passover seder" (GGM, p. 103). (Not after his holding a door for her!) In any case, the podium effect is a principal reason for the erroneously termed "lecherous professor" situation.

Third and finally, let us consider the assertion that the professor "had no intention of doing anything other than using and summarily disposing of her." While I do not wish to approve of professors fornicating with students, it should also be pointed out that most men do not rub their hands like nickelodeon-show villains and cackle: "Heh, heh! I'm going to use this girl to sate my wicked lusts and then abandon her to heartbreak and ruin!" Going into an affair, a man, like a woman, may not even know precisely what he wants or intends. But experience indicates that whenever a love affair does not work out to a woman's perfect satisfaction (which in practice means always), she will be inclined to foist a tendentious and self-exculpating interpretation upon the events: she "loved" him, while he was "just using" her. One of the reasons for the institution of marriage, I have come to believe, is to prevent women from doing this, to enforce public recognition of the legitimacy of a man's taking a mate. Marriage is what lets men say, "It's okay—she's my wife." The sentimental scenario of the heartless cad's "preying upon" the wide-eyed girl is dangerous because it appeals so powerfully both to female passivity and irresponsibility, and to the male protective instinct. Without some socially sanctioned form of sexual union, men's protective urges might go into overdrive and we would see them shooting up the town trying to "protect" young women from becoming mothers.

I have come across male commentators, for example, maintaining that professors who "prey upon" female students should (in certain cases) be treated as rapists. This is a radical departure from the Christian view of women as moral agents, and the high status of women in Western society is essentially bound up with such a view. As far as I can see, if we are unwilling to hold women strictly accountable for their actions, we have only one logical recourse available: a return to the ancient Roman legal doctrine that a woman is a perpetual minor. This would involve an end not merely to contemporary "women's liberation" but to an entire legal tradition that has developed within Christendom over centuries. For starters, it means women could no longer be permitted to hold property or enter into contracts. Although demeaning to women and inconvenient even for men, such a system is at least internally consistent. What is both inconsistent and morally indefensible is what feminism and the misguided gallantry of certain male conservatives are now combining to promote: freedom for women to do as they damned well please, with blame and punishment for men if the women are not happy with the results of their own behavior.

In sum, I would advise men not to let their tears be jerked too easily by stories of women falling helplessly prey to seduction and abandonment. Ever since the day, well before the dawn of history, when human beings first grasped the connection between coitus and childbirth, all societies have demanded sexual self-restraint from their women as a matter of course. It is a highly suspicious circumstance that the most politically "empowered" women in the history of the world have suddenly turned sexually helpless.

Another expression of Shalit's feminine-passive pattern of thinking is that, in emphasizing the reservation of sex for marriage, she says almost nothing about *getting* girls married. Her strategy for them amounts to "some day your prince will come." Since she focuses exclusively upon young women, it is not clear what she would say to the millions of lonely career women who have followed this advice to the letter and "find themselves" being overtaken by menopause still waiting for the tailspinning man of their dreams to appear.

The author quotes with approval a number of allegedly modest young women for saying "I haven't found anyone worth marrying yet." This is not self-respect but self-conceit, and I do not buy it. A man picked randomly off the street today would often be as good as whatever bloke such a girl eventually settles for, assuming she manages to settle in time at all.

Another of Shalit's allegedly modest women says: "I'm abstinent because I have a goal in life. I want to be a doctor or a registered nurse. If I have a baby or something that blocks my goal, I'm not going to be able to achieve that. So being focused and staying in school is my main goal right now." For young women like this, notes Shalit, "having a baby symbolizes being 'stuck'" (GGM, pp. 65-66). The author does not seem to perceive that this is merely feminist careerism and antinatalism as usual, and has nothing to do with modesty.

Women are at the peak of their sexual attractiveness to men in their early twenties for a good reason: this is also the peak of their fertility, which begins a steep, irreversible decline around age 26. Shalit herself apparently delayed marriage until about 28. In parts of Scandinavia—that vanguard of Western decadence—the average age for women at first marriage has now passed 30. One of Shalit's modesty activists had her first child at 37, and she pooh-poohs the woman's friends who had warned of the dangers by simply noting that the baby in this particular case was born healthy. Some years ago, a survey discovered that 89 percent of younger, high-achieving women believe they can safely postpone pregnancy until their forties. In 2002, the American Society for Reproductive Medicine attempted to correct such misconceptions with a campaign of public-service ads; the project was abandoned because of opposition from feminist groups.

In the America of the 1950s—the baby boom—the average age for women at first marriage sank as low as 20. I emphasize the word "average": plenty of girls were younger, marrying right out of high school or even before. To this day, marriage at 16 is legal for girls in all 50 states (with parental consent). During the Christian Middle Ages, a bride was often a bit younger still. Most Americans today have no idea how bizarre their horror at "teenage pregnancy" would have seemed in other times and places.

On a final note, and as a service to my female readers, I would like to reveal what makes a man commit. It is in fact an extremely simple matter, although carefully unmentioned in women's magazines: children. A normal man feels morally committed to a woman who is bearing him children he can feel certain are his. The survival of our civilization may depend upon women's speedily reacquainting themselves with this ancient and timeless reality.

The Last Ditch, March 17, 2008

HOME ECONOMICS

1. TWO CONFLICTING CONCEPTIONS OF FEMININE DIGNITY

One of the hallmarks of Western civilization is the unusually high status it has accorded women. That has often been attributed to the influence of Christianity, which prizes certain typically feminine virtues (mercy, humility) more than pagan society had. But Tacitus had already noted the respect paid to women's opinions as being typical of the pagan Germanic tribes of his time. Some believe the regard paid to women to be a reflection of conditions in ancient Northern Europe, where the nuclear rather than the extended family was the more important economic unit. But however it may have originated, women's position in our civilization has recently been eroded by economic developments and by the feminist movement. The present essay aims to explain how this has happened and argue the need to reverse the process.

Much confusion exists regarding the feminist attack upon women's status, because the feminist movement has always presented itself to outsiders—usually with success—as an effort to improve that status. Feminists, as we all know, assert that women are rightfully the "equals" of men and deserve a "level playing field" on which to compete with them. In our time, it is a rare person whose notions about women's claims remain wholly uninfluenced by these slogans; that is true even of many who think of themselves as opponents of feminism. For example, certain would-be defenders of Western civilization believe Islam presents a danger to us principally because it does not accept "equality of the sexes." Indeed, they sometimes make it sound as though they would have no objection to Islam if only Muslim girls were free to wear miniskirts, join the Army, and divorce their husbands. Or again, many in the growing father's movement describe their goal as implementing "true" equality rather than recovering their traditional role as family heads. I have even known conservatives to earnestly assure young audiences that the idea of sexual equality comes to us from Christianity—a crueler slander upon the Faith than Voltaire or Nietzsche ever imagined. The extreme case of such confusion can be found in "mainstream" conservatives such as William Kristol, who claims to oppose feminism on the grounds that its more exotic manifestations "threaten women's recent gains": in other words, the problem with feminism is that it endangers feminism. It is difficult to combat a movement whose fundamental premises one accepts.

In fact, the high standing of women in our civilization not only long predates feminist ideology but is logically incompatible with it. To understand why, one needs to keep two points in mind: (1) women's traditional status was linked to behavioral expectations—fulfilling the duties of their station; and (2) it assumed qualitative differences and complementarity (rather than "fair" competition) between the sexes.

As to the first point: strictly speaking, it was never women *as such* who enjoyed high status but rather the social roles proper to them—those of wife and mother, chiefly. Being born female (or male) is merely a natural fact of no intrinsic moral significance, but the filling of a social role involves effort and often sacrifice. Accordingly, the respect paid to women was not an unconditional birthright; it was reserved for women who fulfilled their feminine obligations.

Among those obligations, marital fidelity was of supreme importance: so much so that in our language general terms such as virtue and morality have often been used to refer specifically to sexual fidelity in women. That is owing not to irrational prudery, as the apostles of sexual liberation imagined, but to the recognition that all which is necessary to destroy a race and civilization is for its women to refuse to be faithful wives and mothers.

The Western tradition also includes a strong presumption that women wish to fulfill their role; in other words, women are assumed to be "virtuous" until proven otherwise. In certain eras it was dangerous even to suggest that a lady might not be a paragon of sexual self-restraint if one did not have very strong proofs: an aspersion upon a woman's honor was grounds for a duel. Of course, that does not make much sense when women have no honor; and today, the proponents of equality and liberation openly repudiate the very idea as an "oppressive social construct." But to be frank, I suspect honor never was actually the primary determinant of women's behavior. Good example (especially from their mothers), habit, lack of opportunity, religious instruction, and, in the last instance, the prospect of social disgrace and financial ruin were probably always more effective with them.

Men, however, have often been encouraged to believe that women are naturally monogamous, unmotivated by anything so base as sexual attraction, and only seek "good husbands" whom they disinterestedly marry out of love. This pleasing and edifying view of womanhood is the basis of the West's cultural forms surrounding relations between the sexes: gallantry, chivalry, courtship, and companionate marriage. These are what place love, in Edmund Burke's phrase, "if not among the virtues, among the ornaments of life."

There are also certain more practical, if less delicate, considerations involved: viz., if a husband trusts his wife, he can skip rushing home from the office unannounced to make sure she is not in bed with the gardener. That leaves him free to devote his full attention to his own role as breadwinner for children he is sure are his own.

The socially beneficial effects of the chivalrous view of womanhood are quite independent of its accuracy. There is not necessarily any pre-established harmony between what is true and what it is useful for men to believe. A man may be better off not knowing the whole truth about women—even, or perhaps especially, his wife. But most women cooperated enthusiastically in promoting the chivalrous view, even if they were not taken in by it themselves. That is partly because they have been shrewd enough to perceive the advantages of maintaining a high reputation with men and partly because they are naturally more reticent than men about their sexual urges ("modest").

But whether based upon knowledge or pleasing illusion, the regard in which our civilization has held women depends utterly upon their practice of monogamy, and makes no sense apart from it. As long as cases of female adultery were few enough, they could be passed off to men as freaks of nature, akin to two-headed babies. When, on the other hand, wives in their millions act upon the feminist plan of "liberation," walk out on their husbands, separate them from their children, bankrupt them in divorce court, and shack up with other men, that system breaks down. That is where we are today.

To my mind, the most remarkable feature of the revolution we have undergone is the time lag between the changes in women's behavior and changes in men's attitude toward them. Men often strain to blame their own sex for what has gone wrong, though the natural disadvantage of the male's position makes his primary responsibility unlikely on *a priori* grounds: since women have greater control over the mating process, they are inherently likelier than men to be at the root of any fundamental breakdown in family formation and stability.

It seems that many men have an emotional need to believe in the inherent virtue or innocence of women, a bit of sentimentality akin to the Romantics' cult of childhood. Even today, under a burgeoning feminist police-state, male commentators not infrequently berate their own sex for an allegedly insufficient appreciation of the lofty claims of womanhood. The kindest thing one might say of such men is that they are condemning themselves to irrelevance. A somewhat less kind judgment might be that they are collaborators.

The chivalrous view of women is helpful for keeping in check the naturally wayward desires of young husbands in a substantially monogamous society; it is useless or positively harmful in a society being run by spoiled and tyrannical females who have "liberated" themselves from domestic obligations. As usual, conservatives are busy calling for the barn door to be shut long after the horse has run off. Our task today is not to "safeguard" or "protect" marriage but to rebuild it almost from scratch. The strategy for doing so will necessarily be different from the strategy for defending it when it was merely under threat.

2. FEMINISM AS MALE-ROLE-ENVY

Let us now turn to our second point about women's traditional status: namely, that it implied sexual complementarity and cooperation. This means that their status cannot be maintained once complementarity is displaced by a normative ideal of sexual equivalence and competition. The feminist movement has, of course, effected precisely such a displacement, thereby undermining the respect for women they claim to promote. I will now try to explain how that happened.

First, a caveat: most critical discussions of feminism concentrate on refuting its doctrines, such as the ascription of feminine traits to upbringing rather than nature. My approach will be different. While such formal refutation of doctrines is not valueless, it seems to me to mistake the fundamental character of feminism. The feminist movement consists essentially not of ideas at all but of attitudes, or even mere emotions. Feminist "theory," as it is grandiloquently called, is simply whatever the women in the movement come up with in *post facto* justification of their attitudes and emotions. A heavy focus on feminist doctrine seems to me symptomatic of the rationalist fallacy: the assumption that people are motivated primarily by beliefs. If they were, the best way to combat an armed doctrine would indeed be to demonstrate that its beliefs are false. But in the case of feminism, even more than Marxism and other political ideologies, it is rather the beliefs that are motivated by various personal and nonrational needs. I propose, therefore, that feminism may be better understood through a consideration of the feminist herself.

A feminist in the strict and proper sense may be defined as *a woman who envies the male role*.

By the male role I mean, in the first place, providing, protecting, and guiding rather than nurturing and assisting. This in turn involves relative independence, action, and competition in the larger impersonal society outside the family, the use of language for communication and analysis (rather than expressiveness or emotional manipulation), and deliberate behavior aiming at objective achievement (rather than the attainment of pleasant subjective states) and guided by practical reasoning (rather than emotional impulse).

Both feminist and nonfeminist women sense that these characteristically male attributes have a natural primacy over their own. I prefer to speak of "primacy" rather than superiority in this context since both sets of traits are necessary to propagate the race. One sign of male primacy is that envy of the female role by men is virtually nonexistent—even, so far as I know, among homosexuals.

Normal women are attracted to male traits and wish to partner with a man who possesses them. Healthy societies are marked by a cooperative reciprocity between the sexes, but an unequal one in the sense that it involves male leadership of the female, somewhat as in ballroom dancing.

The feminists' response to the primacy of male traits, on the other hand, is a feeling of inadequacy in regard to men—a feeling ill-disguised by defensive assertions of her "equality." She desires to possess masculinity directly, in her own person, rather than partnering with a man. That is what leads her into the spiritual *cul de sac* of envy.

And perhaps even more than she envies the male role itself, the feminist covets the external rewards attached to its successful performance: social status, recognition, power, wealth, and the chance to control wealth directly (rather than be supported). She tends not to give much thought to the great mass of men who struggle to fulfill the demands of their role without ever attaining the rewards of superior performance.

Let us consider next what envy is. First, it involves a painful awareness of something good or desirable in another person. This much it has in common with emulation. The emulator, however, is primarily concerned with self-improvement. Envy has a fundamentally negative character; it wants to bring the other down rather than raise itself up. The envier usually does not admit that explicitly but rather claims to have been cheated, whether by the envied party or by the surrounding society: he disguises his envy as a zeal for justice. Often he claims to want to compete on a level playing field, but maintains that competition has been "fixed."

Envy, however, is distinct from the sense of justice in being fundamentally unappeasable. The righteously indignant person genuinely wants to come to a settlement. By contrast, if the envied party grants what the envier demands, it merely further demonstrates his superiority and provokes more envy. One reason the feminists have gotten as far as they have is that many men are untroubled by envy themselves. These men cannot understand the psychology behind feminism. Sincerely caring about women and wishing to promote their welfare, they waste effort on futile attempts to reason or compromise. They imagine that limited concessions might persuade feminists that men are not really so bad after all.

But it is a metaphysical impossibility to "grant" what a feminist envies: the successful performance of the male role including risk overcome, obstacles surmounted, and objectively verifiable achievement. What the appeasers actually do is grant women some of the external appearances and rewards of such achievement. That is the meaning of corporate hiring and promotional preferences. But a little reflection will reveal why such concessions can never satisfy the feminist. She is humiliated precisely by the awareness that her advancement is an unearned act of charity on the part of the hated "patriarchy." It would be difficult to imagine, in fact, a more efficient means of stoking her frustration and resentment. (The situation with racial preferences, incidentally, is precisely analogous: thus, one book on black beneficiaries of "affirmative action" is aptly titled *The Rage of a Privileged Class*.)

Indeed, concessions are perceived as signs of weakness, and whet the appetite for more concessions, a cycle that could only end with the complete self-destruction of the envied party. In other words, feminists' claim to be motivated by love of justice or fairness is flapdoodle. Feminism is a species not of righteous indignation but of hatred.

In practice, since the feminist can never be the equal of men at the male role, she concentrates her efforts upon sabotaging that role. In other words, because she cannot level up, she contents herself as best she can with leveling down. So the practical consequence of feminist political power is to make it impossible for men to "do their thing" (fulfill their role). For example, women may not be able to have careers as glamorous and successful as they imagined, but one accusation of "harassment" is all it takes to destroy the career of a man whose accomplishments she could never equal. And there is no question that many women get a sadistic pleasure from wielding such power. I myself once heard a woman boast of getting three different men fired.

A whole legal industry has mushroomed within a single generation based upon newly invented crimes and torts of which only men can be guilty and only women can be victims. Obviously, the Western tradition of high regard for women is not going to survive the spread of such behavior indefinitely. Women who wonder why men do not seem to "respect" them any more might seek the answer in the mirror.

Envy of the male role has devastating consequences for women's performance of their own proper role as well. Although it may be a secondary or supporting one in relation to men, it is indispensable for the survival of the race: the woman bears, nurtures, and to a great extent educates the rising generation. The feminist either refuses to fulfill her natural role or at best does so resentfully, sullenly, and poorly. For that reason, feminism should not be treated merely as a personal folly on the part of some misguided or spoiled women—it is a mortal threat to any society in which it truly takes hold. Enemies of heterosexual cooperation and procreation are enemies of the human race.

3. MODERN NEGLECT OF THE ECONOMIC SIDE OF MARRIAGE

Having examined briefly—in the first section—the two principal ways in which feminism has undermined the former position of esteem enjoyed by women in our civilization, let us proceed to consider how that position used to be maintained.

The bedrock of the system, more fundamental than the ideal of chivalry, was the institution of marriage. The strictest possible fulfillment of the conditions of marriage by women is obviously necessary before men can be made to believe that women are ethereally pure, naturally monogamous beings selflessly devoted to the good of their families in a way earthy, lust-filled men cannot comprehend.

Traditional sexual morality can be summed up quite simply: men and (especially) women have a measure of choice in deciding whether or whom to marry, but they are not at liberty to decide for themselves what a marriage is. In other words, we submit ourselves to marriage, which is a timeless institution; we do not adapt it to suit our preferences.

What, then, is a marriage? I define it as *a lifelong sexual and economic union between a man and a woman*. In marriage, a man and woman maintain an exclusive sexual relationship producing (in most cases) children of recognized paternity, and they share productive abilities and resources with a view to rearing their children; and both of these things they do for the term of their natural lives together.

Contrary to the superficial views of many people, particularly women, a wedding is not the defining attribute of marriage: it is merely a ceremony that normally marks a couple's entry into marriage. The only essential purpose of a wedding is to establish paternity, to declare publicly who the presumptive father of the woman's future children is.

Going into a marriage, sex is the woman's strong hand. In early adulthood, when humans normally reproduce, the male sex-drive is incomparably stronger than the female, and the female's sense of shame or modesty is at its height. That is why women rather than men are the primary choosers in the mating dance. But the man is naturally the economically stronger party. As nature made women to be the bearers and nurturers of children, so it made men to be the principal providers for families.

General affluence, female careerism, and hiring preferences for women all erode the man's natural strong point. Furthermore, the modern overstressing of sex and the corresponding neglect of the economics of marriage amount to a focus on the woman's natural strength rather than the man's: the sexual revolution has not strengthened the man's position as popularly advertised, but undermined it.

Let me give an example of the typical modern failure to consider marriage from the economic point of view. Western journalists such as today's propagandists against "Islamofascism" frequently assert that polygamy is morally objectionable because it "demeans women." Typically, they offer no explanation, regarding the matter as self-evident. But it is only the relative prosperity of our society that may make it seem so. Actual polygamous societies tend to be characterized by general poverty, with most of the wealth concentrated in a few male hands. A woman in such a society does not normally face the alternative of two otherwise comparable suitors, one of whom will be faithful to her and the other have a harem. Her choice is likely to be having her fate bound to that of a destitute man or being tolerably supported by a wealthy or powerful man whose attentions she will have to share.

It is by no means self-evident that Western women would reject the possibility of formal polygamy if forced by circumstances to make such a choice; women seek security, and the West's current informal polygamy is in fact a product of women's choices far more than men's. In fact, viewed economically, the function of monogamy is not to improve the condition of women at all, but rather to ensure that relatively poor men are able to father children.

The tendency to disregard the economics of procreation has encouraged many commentators to adopt what might be called a sexual-extortion model of matrimony, i.e., its portrayal as the finagling of a reluctant and grudging "commitment" from a man by means of the threat of sexual frustration: a triumph of the female over the male, rather than the sanctification of their union.

Let us remind ourselves of some obvious facts. Sex has always been available to men outside of marriage by the simple expedient of direct purchase. Prostitutes, no less than wives, are supported by their men. But since the prostitute has numerous "husbands," each one only has to provide a small fraction of her support. This makes prostitution a far better bargain for men than marriage, from the perspective of individual sexual self-interest. If men wanted nothing from women but sexual access, renting beats owning: there is no good reason for them to marry at all.

But what would one say of a man who contentedly consorted with prostitutes without ever feeling that anything was lacking in his erotic life? A certain type of conservative commentator will promptly respond that we must summon the vice squad to arrest the scoundrel; but that would not be an answer to quite the question I mean to pose here. I am not asking what the proper moral judgment upon, or practical response to, such a case would be; I am asking whether it would not be just plain odd —

sexually abnormal—for a man not to sense that marriage had something to offer him that prostitutes did not. Most men would, I think, concur with me in feeling that such a fellow is in a condition analogous to a tone-deaf or color-blind or lobotomized man: something is missing from his perception. The reductively sexual model of matrimony cannot account for this.

Marriage has a number of things to offer men apart from coitus, in fact, but the most important is children. Ours is the only species whose males are conscious of their biological responsibility for particular offspring. The discovery of fatherhood was a watershed event in human history greater than the discovery of the wheel, fire, or agriculture. Civilization is very largely a matter of high-investment parenting, and that requires heavy and continuing paternal involvement. Such involvement rests upon a fundamental anthropological fact: viz., men will gladly work, fight, and sacrifice for children provided they feel sure of their own paternity. No shotgun marriages, no governmental child-support enforcement agencies, not even much in the way of exhortation is necessary for that to occur. The human male finds satisfaction in fatherhood.

But the brute economic reality of procreation is that women and children consume resources that men are called upon to supply. Babies, unlike the young of many beasts, come into the world utterly helpless. And in the late stages of pregnancy, a woman is close to helpless herself, while in the first weeks after childbirth her attention is almost wholly absorbed by her infant. Men pick up the slack. Generally speaking, a woman marries a meal ticket; a man marries trouble and expense. Men understand that. It is the principal reason they are reluctant to "commit," to sign their futures over to women of whose characters and intentions they cannot be certain. Traditionally, men have been rewarded (e.g., with higher social status) for taking on the burden and risk of starting a family. Women, in turn, were expected to remain faithful so that a husband could be sure his labor and resources were not being used to support another man's offspring. Sexual pleasure does not even enter into the matter.

As a counterpiece to the sexual-extortion model, one might easily limn an analogously one-sided, exclusively economic model of marriage, somewhat as follows: a stepmotherly Nature forces men who wish to procreate to purchase a highly fuel-inefficient incubator. Sometimes it turns out to be infertile, but even then it cannot be traded in or returned. One can never even be completely sure the children it produces are his.

That ungallant interpretation of marriage is not an invention of my own misogynistic pen. Something very like it can be found in a host of ancient and medieval writers. The following is taken from the *Hippolytus* of Euripides:

> Women! This coin which men find counterfeit! Why, Lord Zeus, did you put them in the light of the sun? If you were so determined to breed the race of man, the source of it should not have been women: so might we have lived in houses free of the taint of women's presence. But now, to bring this plague into our homes we drain our fortunes. The father who begets her must add a dowry gift to pack her off to another's house and be rid of the load. And he that takes the cursed creature enriches his heart's jewel with dear adornment, beauty heaped on vileness. With lovely clothes the poor wretch tricks her out, spending the wealth that underprops his house. . . .

The passage continues, but you get the idea.

I am aware that many readers will be displeased by the frankness—some might say cynicism—with which I write of these matters. Traditionally, the raw sexual and economic facts of marriage have been politely concealed by superadded ideas such as romantic love and gallantry. In the years following the Second World War, such antiquated fashions were with increasing rudeness torn from the sexual act by fraudulent sex "scientists" and pornographers. But the economic realities have not similarly been dragged into the light of day. On the contrary, our prosperity has made it easy to downplay them even more than in the past.

An example of such polite concealment is found in the traditional etiquette with respect to greeting newly married couples. It was customary to say "congratulations" to the man, but never to the woman; to the bride one offered only "best wishes." The pretense was that the man was receiving an unmerited windfall. The reality, of course, is that the man assumes the principal burden in marriage. For women, it is an economic bonanza.

One factor in the disintegration of marriage and sex roles is that, spoiled by prosperity, women actually came to believe the chivalrous pretense and forgot the underlying economic reality. They expect men to be grateful for the opportunity to support them. (Wendy Shalit is an outstanding example of this mentality.) It is a case of gallantry being abused by its beneficiaries. Under such circumstances, men cannot simply go on behaving in the old manner as though nothing were wrong. It is incumbent upon them to fight back against the forces arrayed against them, in part by emphasizing some home truths about the economic realities of marriage. Perhaps it is time for young men to stop paying for dates and coyly explain that they are "saving their wallets" for marriage. If that sounds cynical to a traditional sensibility, my answer is that such cynicism may simply be the price for reestablishing the natural family as the basis of our civilization.

4. FEMALE ATTRACTION TO "PROVIDERS"

Most men eventually come to the melancholy realization that a woman's choice of mate is largely, and often principally, motivated by economic considerations. In their drive for power, the feminists gave out rosy promises to men that they could change this; that women sought providers only because they were being unfairly barred from the realm of production (which feminists assumed could only lie outside the home). Once women established themselves in the labor force, the pressure upon men to provide for them would be eased. Women would behave less materialistically and choose mates on the basis of personal qualities.

At the same time, and rather inconsistently, women were assured that putting their careers first would incidentally make them eagerly sought out by high-flying men. A popular female self-help book of the early 1980s, for example, was titled *Men Are Just Desserts*.

As usual, the feminists treated as historically conditioned something that was in reality natural. The female tendency to seek provider-mates evolved long before the dawn of history, when economic considerations meant hunting ability and bare survival rather than Sports Utility Vehicles and Hawaiian vacations. Women attracted to men able to provide for offspring had more surviving offspring. So today they are simply hard-wired to seek such men. What actually happens when a woman starts earning $100,000 a year, therefore, is not that she ceases to seek a man who can provide for her but that she perceives men as providers (and hence potential mates) only if they are earning even more. When the feminist project is carried out, the majority of men do not get less-materialistic wives; they simply do not get wives at all.

Even if there were enough wealthy men to go around, such men are rarely interested in marrying the corporate spinsters frantically pursuing them. That leads to a kind of tragicomic situation. There exists today a whole genre of self-help literature aimed at well-to-do professional women, promising to show them, as one author phrases it, "how to flatter, tease, dupe, and otherwise manipulate a man into marriage." A company in Manhattan charges such women $9,600 for a beauty and personality makeover that culminates in a make-believe wedding. The ersatz ceremonies are often impossible to complete because the "brides" break down crying. Professionally successful men, for their part, are starting to report frequent nuisance calls from dating agencies on behalf of these desperate women.

Obviously, most of those women are going to fail in their quest no matter how many self-help books they read or how much money they spend. There is still a boy for every girl in the world, but there is not a *higher-status* boy for every menopausal career girl who foolishly sacrificed her nubile years to achieving wealth and status for herself. These women, in other words, are victims of their own success; their lives are what they have made them. To paraphrase Oscar Wilde: a man would need a heart of stone to behold their situation without laughing.

In an affluent society, even men of well-below-average provisioning capability can easily reproduce at above replacement rate. They may, for that matter, be better husbands and fathers than most wealthy men. Considered rationally, therefore, general prosperity ought to lead to a flourishing society of moderately large families. But the female sex instinct, as the reader may possibly have noticed, is not rational. It is triggered by relative rather than absolute wealth, and so men's sexual attractiveness is still determined by their status within the social hierarchy as perceived by women.

Another factor now working against the marital prospects of ordinary men is the influence of "romantic" books and movies upon women's imaginations.

Hollywood comedy, for example, has long pandered to the primitive female instinct to seek a mate with limitless provisioning capability. A stock hero is the handsome, jet-setting bachelor. His wealth is simply there, without his needing to go to any trouble to acquire it, leaving him free to devote full attention to romancing the heroine.

In *That Touch of Mink* (1962), Cary Grant flies Doris Day to Philadelphia in his private jet for a plate of fettuccini. She tags along as he addresses the UN. They go to a Yankees game and sit in the dugout with the players (he owns the team, apparently). He furnishes her with a new wardrobe complete with private fashion show. He buys up all the tickets on a peak-season flight to Bermuda so she can have the airplane to herself. None of this fantasy is based upon the heroine's rational concern that the children be adequately provided for; it is pure female luxury. Grant is played off against a "creepy" rival whose unworthiness consists in his having to hold down an ordinary office job, vacationing in East New Jersey instead of Bermuda, and dining on TV dinners and inexpensive wine.

This movie, along with the many others like it, actually gets cited as an example of wholesome entertainment from a more innocent age. The average dull-witted conservative media critic cannot perceive anything objectionable since there is no explicit or extramarital sex. In fact, such "romantic" pictures amount to a kind of gold digger's pornography. In contrast to Jane Austen's plot lines, where real risks and difficulties are encountered and moral lessons can be learned, these movies are mere wish fulfillment. They set women up for disappointment by teaching them to have unrealistic expectations about love and life. And, of course, they create absurdly unattainable standards for men.

Or consider the related phenomenon of pulp romance fiction. The market for such books mysteriously exploded around the same time women began entering the workforce in large numbers. The pioneering company, Harlequin Enterprises Ltd., saw its earnings grow two-hundredfold in the decade of the 1970s. Today, Harlequin has many competitors, and some sources report that the romance genre accounts for over half of paperback sales in the United States. The lesson to be drawn, it seems, is that when women become able to provide for themselves, they do not cease to think about men; instead, marriage to a real but imperfect provider is replaced by endless fantasizing about being swept up into the arms of impossibly perfect provider-mates. I once knew a professionally successful registered nurse who owned thousands of those books; the walls of every room in her house were lined with them. She must have read them every waking hour not devoted to working or eating. Not coincidentally, she had neither husband nor children.

Warren Farrell explained as early as 1986 why such literature is the functional equivalent of pornography for women. But while a great deal has been written to deplore the spread of pornography in our society, almost no serious attention has been directed to the causes and effects of romance fiction. My hunch is that its influence is actually more pernicious than pornography, because women have so much greater natural power than men to determine real-world courtship and marriage patterns.

5. NO PROPERTY RIGHTS WITHIN THE TRADITIONAL FAMILY

Male provisioning may have arisen as an adaptation by early hominids to the more adverse climatic conditions they encountered upon migrating out of Africa. To this day, female food production remains the rule in much of black Africa. The harsher climate of Eurasia, especially in its more northerly regions, is what requires male physical strength and foresight along with their female counterpart: more intensive nurturance of children.

Anthropologists have suggested that better use of the sexual division of labor may even be what gave modern humans the decisive competitive advantage over Neanderthals. I would not wish to place too much weight upon an emergent and possibly untestable theory. But for many years, critics of feminism have been routinely dismissed as Neanderthals and Cavemen. It would be a gratifying vindication for us should it turn out that man's more primitive predecessors actually became extinct through "equality in the workplace." (It is also amusing to consider how our pampered feminists might have fared in the "hostile work environment" of the Middle Paleolithic.)

Although originating in response to difficult natural conditions, the practice of male provisioning survived into the era of diminished scarcity following the end of the last Ice Age and the rise of settled agriculture. That is what first allowed for capital accumulation, an essential precondition of civilization. We are fortunate indeed that the men of ancient Mesopotamia had no feminists around to convince them it was "sexist" to deny property rights to their wives. Those who generate wealth have a better idea of its value than those who are supported by others. It is doubtful whether civilization could have arisen with women in control of the prehistoric purse strings.

Few things generate more feminist ire than this traditional absence of female property rights within the family. Such retrospective indignation, however, is merely another example of the misunderstandings that can arise from not having to look harsh economic realities in the face.

The father, in his role as provider, had a *duty* to manage his family's property for the long-term benefit of the family as a whole (including, of course, his wife). A man's right to control the allotment of the wealth he himself produced was essentially tied to that obligation. Feminists, as usual, perceive only the man's rights and not the responsibilities from which they derived.

The sexes have not changed much since the Neolithic age, even if our ideas about "rights" have. Even today one can find men with six-figure salaries who cannot get out of debt. They do not live beyond their means; their wives do. In Schopenhauer's words, "Women think men are intended to earn money so that they may spend it." One of the traditional goals of rearing daughters has been precisely to disabuse them of this "natural" feminine way of thinking.

The consequences of failing to do so may be seen in certain recent developments in Europe. In 1999, a female British Labour Party politician announced plans "to compel employers to pay men's wages into their wives' bank accounts. . . . Wives will have sole discretion over whether or not they receive their husband's wages directly." Meanwhile, in Germany a law has been proposed that "would require husbands to pay pocket money to their wives. Failure to pay pocket money . . . could result in the offender being hauled into family court and ordered to pay."

By contrast, the traditional housewife, besides being grateful for her husband's support and frugal with his resources, was expected to make her own contribution to the household:

> She seeks wool and flax, and works with willing hands. She rises while it is yet night and provides food for her household and tasks for her maidens. Her lamp does not go out at night. She puts her hands to the distaff. She looks well to the ways of her household, and does not eat the bread of idleness.

Such are the attributes of the good wife as described in Proverbs 31 (following the wistful question, "A good wife who can find?"). In other words, it is in no way an innovation of feminism that women should carry out economic functions.

But that is quite different from having a career for the purpose of "self-realization." A woman's traditional economic role is "family realization." A woman dedicated to fulfilling that role might have been bewildered as to how she would benefit from property rights that were legally enforceable against other members of her own family.

6. FAMILY AS THE PRIMAL FORM OF COMMUNITY

While the economic aspect of marriage is badly neglected today, we are hardly uninterested in economic matters *per se*. On the contrary, money may be the one thing modern man obsesses over as much as sex. Our economic concerns, however, are concentrated on success and consumption in the market rather than on providing for home and children. That is remarkable, because the primary reason men have traditionally pursued wealth in the first place is that they have families to support (or wish to have them).

Elementary economics textbooks dutifully inform students that the word economy comes from the Greek term for household management. But no significance is attributed to that bit of information, and it may be the last time a student of economics ever hears households mentioned. "Economy" can still be found employed in its original domestic sense by Samuel Johnson and other 18th-century writers. Only gradually was its meaning extended metaphorically into "political economy," the household management of the entire state, as it were. Once political economy had become a recognized discipline, "political" was dropped from the name as cumbersome and unnecessary to make the speaker's meaning clear. Subsequently, the original sense faded from men's minds. Factories and banks, not homes, came to be thought of as the principal settings of "economic" activity. Today we see journalists sloppily referring to the securities market as "the economy." So completely has the market driven out consideration of the household that one economist, Gary Becker, has recently used marginal-utility theory in attempting to reinterpret the natural family itself as being the result of economically rational calculation.

There is something quite odd about trying to explain the primary and natural fact of procreation by means of the secondary and derivative behavior of the market. Consider, for example, the observable fact that many parents willingly risk their lives to protect their offspring. Such self-sacrificial behavior might be called *transeconomic*. People will not do that sort of thing for merely economic goods. (The stories of men jumping from hotel windows following the 1929 stock-market crash, by the way, originated in a comedy routine of the time.) While people "value" both resources and children, the two classes of goods seem to be incommensurable. Families are in large part the purpose of wealth.

The sale of children, indeed, is not unknown among the desperately poor. But the difficult question for any exclusively economic analysis would be to explain why such a practice is not normal and universal; children most certainly consume enough resources to raise issues of "cost effectiveness." The present writer hopes human beings never become *that* rational.

The economy of the home differs qualitatively as well as quantitatively from that of commercial enterprises or nations. The family actually does operate roughly according to the principle "from each according to his abilities; to each according to his needs." This communist slogan is not, in other words, intrinsically utopian; it is only utopian to extend the principle universally, in defiance of the ineliminable qualitative differences between the natural family and political society. (Many socialist writers lose sight of the familial inspiration of their ideal, but in the original socialist utopia described in Plato's *Republic*, Socrates explicitly recognizes that he is extending the preexisting familial principle to the polis.)

A second difference is that the home does not have a money economy. When the housewife of old spun wool to make clothing for her family, she was creating wealth—adding human value to raw materials—but the wealth found no monetary or numerical expression. So she could not calculate inputs and outputs, or the return on her invested labor. For that reason, muddle-headed feminists refer to the premodern woman's domestic labor as "unpaid."

Clearly, the traditional domestic economy was not "capitalist." But what was it?

The German sociologist Ferdinand Tönnies (1855-1936) famously distinguished two fundamental types of human connectedness: society and community. Of these, community is both conceptually and historically prior. It is characterized by ascribed (i.e., unchosen) statuses, affective attachments to persons and places, strong habits and traditions, and a common worship. Work within a community is understood in the Aristotelian sense of *energeia*, as the realization of a natural potency, the carrying out of a meaningful task or vocation. The family is the prototype of all community.

Society is characterized by chosen or achieved statuses, self-interest, individualism, impersonality, contract, and competition. Work is understood not as a calling but as a "job," an unpleasantness to be endured for the sake of extrinsic rewards such as money and status. The particular nature of the enterprise in which one competes may be a matter of indifference (e.g., dope-dealing being as good as agriculture). The commercial enterprise is the textbook example of a society understood by way of contrast to a community.

Communities such as families, family-based small businesses, villages, and religious congregations are the natural nurseries of larger and looser societies such as cities and large-scale business corporations: societies presuppose communities in a way communities do not presuppose societies. But even as society arises out of community, it has an inherent tendency to erode the natural soil from which it grew. Advanced societies are often marked by a nostalgic "quest for community," in Robert Nisbet's phrase, but members of such societies often fail to appreciate that a return to community would necessarily entail a sacrifice in freedom of personal action—and possibly in material standard of living as well. These are the waters in which cult leaders and demagogues fish. Prominent among such false prophets in recent times have been feminists, calling the duties of married life "slavery" when they are in reality the indispensable basis for the family, and therefore of all real community.

Tönnies himself saw that his typological distinction is not sexually neutral: men can thrive in loose, competitive societies; women generally do not, or, if they do, they lose their femininity in the process. In prefeminist America, we may note, comfortably supported women with time on their hands often did volunteer work in their communities. Nothing is more foreign and terrible to a woman's original inborn nature, observed Tönnies, than trade, than independence as a contracting party and possessor of money. (Supporting a wife need not, be it noted, involve giving her money.) Conversely, nothing has been a greater factor in the modern encroachment of society upon community than the emancipation of women from communal bonds and pursuits.

My citation of a 19th-century sociologist to clarify the nature of the family, by the way, would probably have bewildered Tönnies himself. He could safely assume his readers already knew what a family was, and he used the concept to clarify the nature of other communities. But today, after several decades of a state-sponsored cult of individual gratification, Western Man might just require a course in sociology to grasp matters that the rest of the world has always considered too natural and obvious for explanation.

7. CONSEQUENCES OF UNLIMITED CHOICE

Most leftist utopias involve enjoying all the benefits of tightly knit communities while paying none of the costs in individual freedom such communities demand. Thus, feminists propose to liberate women from "domestic drudgery" and replace it with unrestricted personal choice. Yet the drudgery of marriage and its duties are, quite obviously, the indispensable basis of the family, the model and source for all real community.

It is true that there is a measure of free choice even in marriage: a woman may choose whether, and to a certain extent whom, she will marry. But once a woman makes her choice by taking the vow and entering into the covenant, she *ipso facto* no longer has a choice (just as one cannot eat a cake and have it). In other words, marriage is a one-way nonrefundable ticket. Her husband is her choice even if he eventually displeases her in certain ways, as all mortal husbands necessarily must. When a woman keeps her choice of mate open forever, it is called "spinsterhood."

Ultimately, the fantasies of feminism and sexual liberation rest upon a metaphysical confusion that might be called the *absolutizing of choice*. The illusion is that society could somehow be ordered to allow women to choose without thereby diminishing their future options. Birth control, abortion, the destigmatizing of fornication and lesbianism, the "right" to a career, arbitrary and unilateral divorce — all these have been pitched to women as ways of expanding their choices.

Now, I am in favor of giving women all the choice they can stand. (At present, I think they have rather more than that.) But a careful analysis will reveal that the term has distinct and partly contradictory senses that may not be equally applicable in all contexts. Choice is not a single thing that can be expanded indefinitely at no cost, and a specious appearance of more of it in one area can be shown to entail reducing one's possibilities in another.

One perfectly legitimate sense of choosing is doing as one desires. When we are asked, for example, to choose a flavor of ice cream, all that is meant is a decision as to which would be the most pleasing to us at the moment. That is because the alternative of chocolate or strawberry involves no deep, long-term consequences. But not all choices can be like that.

Consider, for example, a young man's choice of vocation. One of the charms of youth is that it is a time when possibility overshadows actuality. One might become a brain surgeon, or a mountain climber, or a poet, or a statesman, or a monk. It is natural and good for boys to dream about all the various things they might become, but such daydreams can breed a dangerous illusion: that, where anything is still possible, everything will be possible. That is true only in the case of trivial and inconsequential matters. It is possible to sample all of Baskin-Robbins's 31 flavors on 31 successive days. But it is not possible to become a brain surgeon *and* a mountain climber *and* a poet *and* a statesman *and* a monk. A man who tries to do so will only fail in all his endeavors. The reason, of course, is that important enterprises demand large amounts of time and dedication, but the men who undertake them are mortal.

For every possibility we realize, there will be a hundred we must leave forever unrealized; for every path we choose to take, there will be a hundred we must forever renounce. The need for choice in this sense is what gives human life much of its seriousness and much of its poignancy. Those who drift from one thing to another, unable to make up their minds or finish anything they have begun, reveal thereby that they do not grasp an essential truth about the human condition. They are like children who do not wish to grow up.

A woman's sexual choices are analogous to a man's in regard to his calling. Inherently, they cannot be made as easy and reversible as choosing flavors of ice cream. But making them so is what feminism and sexual liberation attempt to do. The underlying motive seems to be precisely a fear of difficult choices and a desire to eliminate the need for them. For example, a woman does not have to think about a man's qualifications to be a father to her children if a pill or a routine medical procedure can remove that possibility. There is no reason to consider carefully the alternative between career and marriage if motherhood can be safely postponed until the age of 40 (as large numbers of women now apparently believe). What we have here is not a clear gain in the *amount* of choice, but a shift from one sense of the word to another—from serious, reflective commitment to merely doing as one desires at any given time. Like the dilettante who dabbles in five professions without finally pursuing any, the liberated woman wants to keep all her options open forever: she wants eternal youth.

The attempt to realize a utopia of limitless choice in the real world has certain predictable negative consequences: notably, it makes women's experience of love one of repeated failure. The liberated woman who rejects both committed marriage and committed celibacy drifts into and out of a series of what are called "relationships," either abandoning or being abandoned by her man (in her mind, it is his fault in both cases). A popular German novel satirizing this pattern of behavior is titled *With the Next Man Everything Will Be Different.*

The lesson inevitably taught by such experiences is that love does not last, that people are not reliable, that in the end one has only oneself to fall back on, that prudence dictates always looking out for number one. And that in turn destroys the generosity, loyalty, and trust that are indispensable if love is to succeed and endure.

The women who have obeyed the new commandment to follow all of their heart's desire do not appear to me to be reveling in a garden of earthly delights. Instead I am reminded of the sad characters from the pages of Chekhov: sleepwalking through life, forever hoping that tomorrow things will somehow be changed for the better as they blindly allow opportunities for lasting happiness to slip through their fingers. But this is merely the natural outcome of conceiving of a human life as a series of revocable and inconsequential choices. We are, indeed, protected from certain risks, but we have correspondingly little to gain; we have fewer worries but no great aspirations. The price we pay for eliminating the dangers of intimacy is eliminating its seriousness.

In place of family formation, we find a "dating scene" without any clear goal, in which men and women are both consumed with the effort to get the other party to close options ("commit") while keeping their own open. There is a hectic and never-ending jockeying for position: fighting off the competition on the one hand, keeping an eye out for a better deal elsewhere on the other. The latest "singles" fad is something called speed dating, where men and women interact for three minutes, then go on to someone else in response to the sound of a bell.

But the real *nec plus ultra* of current tendencies can be seen in certain college "harassment" policies that warn that a "sexual contact" (as it is exquisitely termed) creates no presumption that there will be further "contacts." Apparently, you are guilty of harassing your "sex partner" if you presume otherwise. Committees are being set up to enforce this stuff. It would appear to be based upon the practice in homosexual bathhouses, but it is now being forced upon young men and women as the normative ideal to replace marriage. We behold the self-centered pursuit of short-term pleasure claiming the moral high ground against self-control and lifelong devotion to family. As usual, those unable to govern their own desires have the greatest will to tyrannize over others.

8. MARRIAGE AS AN IRREVERSIBLE COVENANT

Sex belongs to one transient phase of human life, viz., early adulthood. It is futile to attempt to abstract it from its natural and limited place in the life cycle and make it an end in itself. Sustainable civilization requires that more important long-term desires be given preference over short-term wishes that conflict with them, such as the impulse to commit fornication.

The purpose of marriage is not to place shackles upon people or reduce their options, but to enable them to achieve something that most are simply too weak to achieve without the aid of such an institution. Certain valuable things require time to ripen, and you cannot discover them unless you are patient and faithful to your task. Marriage is what tells people to stick to it long enough to find out what happens. Struggling with such difficulties — and even periods of outright discouragement — is part of what allows the desires of men and women to mature and come into focus. Older couples who have successfully raised children together, and are rewarded by seeing them marry and produce children of their own, are unlikely to view their honeymoon as the most important event of their marriage.

People cannot know what they want when they are young. A young man may imagine happiness to consist in living on Calypso's Island, giving himself over to sexual pleasure without ever incurring family obligations; but, like Ulysses, he would eventually find such a life unsatisfying.

Such confusion about one's desires is probably greater in the female, however. For that reason, it is misleading to speak, as old-fashioned men like to do, of young women "wanting marriage." A young woman leafing through the pages of Modern Bride does not yet know what marriage is; all she wants is to have her wedding day and live happily ever after. She may well not have the slightest notion of the duties she will be taking on.

Marriage is often said to exist for the protection of women, and certainly the male protective instinct is much in evidence in most male criticism of the sexual revolution. Principally, however, what they need protecting from is not men intent upon one-night stands — it is their own irrationality, irresponsibility, immaturity, and short-sightedness. One might even legitimately speak of a need to protect women from the delusions of feminism and liberation.

Motherhood is what really forces young women to grow up; I have heard women themselves remark upon this. Scatterbrained dopes whose biggest concern used to be which new hairstyle to try next find themselves keeping accurate financial records and planning their actions, suddenly aware that they have a genuinely important task to perform and surprised to find themselves equal to it.

But without the understanding that marriage is an inherently irreversible covenant, both men and women succumb to the illusion that divorce will solve the "problem" of dissatisfaction in marriage. They behave like the farmer who clears, plows, and plants a field only to throw up his hands on the first really hot and sweaty day of work, exclaiming: "Farming is no fun! I'm going to do something else!" And like that farmer, they have no one to blame but themselves when they fail to harvest any crop.

Understanding the marriage bond as an irreversible covenant similarly influences the way economic activity and property are understood. Rather than being a series of short-term responses to circumstance, labor and investment become an aspect of family life transcending the natural life span of any individual. From a mere means to consumption, wealth becomes a family inheritance. In Burke's fine words: "The power of perpetuating our property in our families is one of the most valuable and interesting circumstances belonging to it, and that which tends most to the perpetuation of society itself. It makes our weakness subservient to our virtue; it grafts benevolence even upon avarice." By contrast, the characteristically modern view of property finds its clearest expression in the title of a bestselling 1998 financial planning guide: *Die Broke*.

9. MODERNITY NATURALLY ERODES MALE ROLES

Obviously the restoration of the marriage covenant is a necessary condition for the restoration of the family and any sustainable civilization. But is it also sufficient? Many female commentators assume so. This, I believe, is because women are naturally programmed to play what Michelle Langley, in her book *Women's Infidelity*, calls "the commitment game." They naturally see "getting him to marry me" as the entire goal of dating and courtship. Accordingly, they focus on their dissatisfaction as the cohabiting girlfriend, and call marriage a "simple solution" to the problem.

I disagree. The rate of female-initiated divorce is conclusive proof that dragging or driving the selfish bastards to the altar is not going to solve anything. As men vainly try to explain to their girlfriends, a marriage ceremony in and of itself changes nothing, and certainly does not cause anyone to "live happily ever after." Today, in fact, much of the same confusion and aimlessness observable on the dating scene is found in family life itself. The deeper problem, as I see it, is an *atrophy of function*.

People join together not simply to be together but to do things they cannot do alone. Traditionally, they have formed families to carry out the essential function of childrearing— along with various economic tasks subordinate to that end, and some secondary functions such as care of the elderly. Conversely, to remain strong, the family must retain some of those functions. Today, however, a father's upper-body strength is no longer needed to provide for children; his personal courage is seldom called upon to protect them. A mother can get clothing and even prepared food from stores more easily than produce those things at home. In other words, the domestic economy has been "outsourced."

As its economic functions wither, the family's sense of community fades: homes turn into warehouses for corporate "human resources" (telling phrase!) and nurseries for public school system fodder. The ancestral hearth becomes a suburban tract house, a site for eating, sleeping, and—decreasingly— procreation. These in turn lose their human (and, indeed, sacramental) significance and become merely animal functions. Leisure activity is replaced by the passivity of diversions such as television or music-listening that involve no interaction between family members. Child psychologists distinguish a phase of "parallel play" before children discover that cooperation will enable them to do more interesting things: our families might be seen as reverting to the parallel-play stage.

These developments are economic in the most proper sense of the term, for the family is still a more fundamental economic fact than the market where goods and services are exchanged. Most professional economists, however, find no place in their thoughts for procreation, or even for sexual dimorphism. And I do not believe that results from the direct influence of anti-natalist or feminist ideology, in which most of them take no interest. It is rather that the home has simply fallen out of the economist's purview.

For example, economists have produced cogent refutations of the feminist "57 cents on the dollar" canard, critiques of "comparable worth," "affirmative action," and so on. But they usually limit themselves to pointing out why men are more productive, i.e., why men's labor commands a higher price on the market than women's. They seem to accept the premise that women and men are interchangeable agents of production whose efficiency can be arithmetically assessed; they ignore qualitative social-role differentiation. That tends not only to undermine the dignity of the traditional female role of wife and mother, as gallant conservatives have long pointed out, but also the specifically male breadwinning role. For men are not simply more productive than women (although they are that as well); they also have a natural provider *role* with social and familial meaning.

The economy is not Wall Street; it is Dad dragging himself out of bed at six o'clock in the morning to go to an unglamorous job because he loves his children. It is a remarkable psychological fact that most men find satisfaction in providing for their families. They certainly do not take much satisfaction in paying income tax or meeting car payments. Children are frequently more expensive than taxes or cars, but most fathers take well to the provider role. Family life transforms what might otherwise be mere drudgery into a vocation; the father's work acquires a significance it cannot have for a bachelor. Is there not something missing from a science of economics that has no use for this fact?

It is, therefore, an insufficient response to the feminist slogan of equal pay for equal work to show that women are not doing equal work. We will eventually have to rediscover the forgotten concept of the "family income" — not only because men usually happen to be better providers than women, but also because the male role is vulnerable in the modern world, and must be shored up for the family to function properly.

The contemporary workplace is inherently unfavorable to men for a number of reasons unrelated to the direct influence of feminism. While classical capitalism of the sort celebrated by the followers of Adam Smith or Ludwig von Mises may not quite have been the Wild West, it did allow significant scope for such male traits as competitiveness, risk-taking, leadership, enterprise, and initiative. In a postindustrial bureaucratic corporation there is little room for any of these. The same psychological traits that once made women better at knitting than men, viz., a high degree of tolerance for routine and repetition, today give them an edge in common forms of employment such as word processing and data entry.

Similarly, the superior social skills that once fitted women to be hostesses now give them an advantage in the expanding customer-service sector of the economy.

Modern machines have lowered the economic value of upper-body strength while increasing that of multi-tasking skills. Women are natural multi-taskers. That is an evolutionary adaptation to the requirements of motherhood, well characterized by antifeminist Carolyn Graglia as a "cheerful responsiveness to constant interruptions." If the male inventors of our labor-saving office devices had known what trouble they were preparing for their grandsons, they might have become Luddites.

Government regulations have grown in such luxurious profusion that, as one executive put it, "We are no longer in business; we are only in compliance." Women are better suited than men to fastidious compliance with bureaucratic directives and regulatory minutiæ. They are usually untroubled by the enforced niceness of Political Correctness, such as governmental sanctions against anyone who forgets to call cripples "the differently abled."

The contemporary white-collar employee is dependent upon a boss for his livelihood, and must therefore be deferential, diplomatic, and often less than forthright about what he thinks. It is not hard to see which sex is better at this sort of behavior. Women are cunning and play their cards close to their chest: an evolutionary adaptation left over from the days when their survival and reproductive success depended on an ability to manipulate males physically stronger than themselves. Today, it makes them naturals at office politics.

Most men find the atmosphere of the modern workplace stifling and tedious, and women themselves are seldom attracted to the sort of docile, gelded drudges that manage to succeed in it. But men cannot find refuge at home either, because the women who might have made homes for them are out competing against them in the activities of the broader society.

10. FEMINISM DELIBERATELY ERODES MALE ROLES

To these intrinsic male disadvantages in the modern workplace must be added those directly created by feminism.

British philosopher C. E. M. Joad once characterized cultural decadence as "a sign of man's tendency to misread his position in the universe, to take a view of his status and prospects more exalted than the facts warrant and to conduct his societies and to plan his future on the basis of this misreading." Feminism might usefully be viewed in this light as the decadence of European womanhood. It can only have been such a delusion of grandeur that led women with no experience of the world of industry to assert their "right" to a career—meaning, really, an easy and successful career. They pictured themselves, feet up on mahogany desks, barking orders at cringing male subordinates, and getting rewarded for it with fat paychecks and prestige.

The practical result of loudly proclaiming that careers will be opened to talents, as students of the "civil rights" movement know, is that vast hordes of formerly contented mediocrities start thinking of themselves as talented. When they fail at their endeavors, they feel cheated, assume someone else must be to blame, and call for punishment.

The gullible women who entered the workforce at the urging of feminists quickly discovered that they did not like it very much (despite their feminine advantages enumerated above). Work turned out to be . . . well, a lot of *work*. Their response to the broken promises of feminism, however, was not to blame the ideologues for having made them or themselves for having believed them; it was to blame men. Men simply had to re-engineer the world of work until women found it "fulfilling." And feminism would lead the way again. (One of the movement's greatest strengths has been this ability to profit politically from its own failures.)

It would be difficult to calculate the number of laws and regulations promulgated in the last three decades with a view to the convenience of working women. And, although feminists have

formulated the proposals, it is largely men who have imple-
mented and enforced them—serenely confident, no doubt, that
the new rules could only be used against *bad* men. But I am
afraid women are no exception to the rule that power corrupts,
and few of them hesitate to convert the novel legal protections
into weapons the moment they sense it might be to their personal advantage.

At my own place of work there are posters prominently dis-
played to inform women of a toll-free number they can call if
they dislike anything a male coworker does or says. There is no
equivalent number for men, obviously; but even if there were, it
is not hard to see which sex is more given to complaining. Other
posters warn men against making any criticism, even casually
and informally, of a woman's job performance.

Everyone knows what is going on, but no one says anything.
The women have all read the stories about $6 million harass-
ment settlements, and figure it beats working for $17 an hour.
Their eyes are peeled for opportunities. The average corporate
manager will unhesitatingly betray a fellow male employee (and
smugly pose as a defender of wronged womanhood) in order to
avoid a lawsuit, and both male and female employees know it.

"Gender equity goals," direct preferences for women in hiring and promotions, are established by corporations in order to
avoid being dragged into court by the EEOC. The public pretense is that women are "advancing" in the workplace; in fact,
they are being artificially hoisted on the backs of men. One of the
most obnoxious aspects of the situation, to my mind, is the sug-
ary rhetoric everywhere used to justify and conceal a reality of
intimidation, cowardice, and injustice.

The feminists have undoubtedly made great advances toward achieving their economic aims. Wages of full-time year-
round male workers in the United States have remained flat
since 1973. In that year, full-time working women's wages were
57 percent those of men; by 2005, they were "earning" (in a
manner of speaking) 77 percent as much as men. The men, of
course, need that money to start or maintain families; the wom-
en do not. Antifeminist women once warned that if their husbands' family-wage jobs were engrossed by spinsters the money

would get wasted on clothing, cosmetics, entertainment, travel, and other frivolities. I do not have hard data on that, but certainly consumer-savings rates in general are extremely low today: it would be worthwhile to disaggregate the figures by sex. One thing no economist will ever tell us, however, is how many babies have not been born thanks to women's workplace "advances."

Another consideration that must temper our enthusiasm for these "advances" is the tax increases we have, not coincidentally, suffered during the same period. Shrewd observers have long understood the natural alliance between feminists wanting to nudge or compel women into the workplace and rapacious government wanting to tax their earnings. It is another instance of the common symbiosis between self-indulgence and despotism, the divide-and-rule principle applied to the family.

Finally, one of the great suppressed realities of the contemporary workplace is the widespread existence of mother guilt in female employees: pangs of conscience brought on by leaving their children to the care of paid surrogates out of a misguided belief that they are "supposed to" keep up with men by holding down full-time jobs. This probably contributes to the notorious personal unpleasantness of many working women, and it certainly affects their job performance.

Apparently it is not as easy to find examples of stay-at-home mothers torn up at the thought of multinational conglomerates deprived of their love and comforting.

11. PRACTICAL CONSEQUENCES OF DOMESTIC ANDROGYNY AND ROLE-REVERSAL

Feminists by preference focus on workplace issues, since their envy is directed at the primary male provider role. But they also have a program for revolutionizing our domestic lives: they call it "sharing the housework."

That may not sound particularly alarming to those still unaware that Spain has already passed a law providing for the arrest of men who fail to do half the housework. Similar moves are afoot in Germany. One wonders what action the international sisterhood will suggest against the men now opting for bachelorhood: conscripting them to serve as butlers for lesbians, perhaps?

Long before resorting to coercion, however, feminists made a pitch for androgyny in the home. It was aimed at both men and women. The principal bait to women involved a promised 50 percent reduction in their housework—undoubtedly appealing on a first hearing. But men, too, were offered rosy prospects: having to bring home only half the bacon, and getting more time with their children. What sort of unfeeling beast could object to a proposal that would allow him to be a better father?

As today's resort to police-state measures makes clear, however, things have not quite worked out as we were led to expect. What went wrong?

One way to find out might be to study actual families that operate on feminist principles. The difficulty seems to lie in locating any. One researcher succeeded in finding a man who did half the infant care—an academic with an ideological commitment to feminism:

> [She] found that he came up with "tricks" for getting through extended contact with his son [such as] "toys and events which kept the baby distracted, and thus decreased the father's level of attention." The father told about trying "to get things done." He couldn't stand the crying and fussing. Sometimes he would "go pound his fist in the wall."

Even when "nontraditional" families turn up, they often do not stick around long enough to be studied. One group of researchers "found on follow-up, just two years later, that only one-quarter of [the families] were maintaining their nontraditional ways."

The reality seems to be that families sometimes resort to androgyny or outright role reversal under conditions of stress (e.g., loss of the father's job or the prolonged illness of the mother), or occasionally as a direct result of ideological commitment, but that they show a strong tendency to return to natural norms over time.

Accepting that natural and permanent sex roles exist, be it noted, need not imply that a father must never feed the baby even if the mother is in a coma. Sex roles have never been quite as carved in stone as feminists sometimes like to make out, and part of the advantage of family life over celibacy is the flexibility it permits in meeting unforeseen challenges.

Feminist observer Janet Steil found, however, that "couples will go to great lengths to conceal a high-earning wife's income to protect the husband's status as primary provider." There is a sound reason for that: overt, prolonged role reversal is fatal to marriage. Researcher Liz Gallese thought she had finally found an example of a happy role-reversal marriage: the wife's career was more successful than the husband's, so he began looking after their child to let her focus on work (the economically rational thing to do). The woman seemed proud of her accomplishments and happy with the arrangement; and Gallese must have thought she had a bestseller on her hands. The reality came to light only when she began speaking to the husband. It turns out that the couple had entirely ceased having sexual relations. Armed with that new information, Gallese began probing more deeply into the wife's sentiments. The woman eventually admitted she wanted another child, but—not by her husband.

"I absolutely refuse to sleep with that man," she declared; "I'll never have sex with him again." Instead, she was now flirting with other successful businessmen. She did not *divorce* her husband, however; he was still too useful as a nanny for the child. Such would appear to be the thanks men can expect for accommodating their wife's career and "sharing the housework."

Since empirical research into androgynous marriage and parenting is limited by a relative scarcity of material for study, let us try a second approach. I suggest that the futility of the feminist "share the housework" project might be clarified by means of the economist's concept of a demand schedule. Everyone values certain things more highly than others, and men and women tend to put the goods they desire in a different order of priority. One unusually perceptive woman has written: "When I want my husband to do 'his half' of household chores, what I really want is for him to do half of everything on my list of important things. But he has his own list."

For example, some men will contentedly allow dirty dishes to pile up into the sink for days but insist that the yard must look like the putting greens at Augusta. From that alone it should be obvious why the feminist proposal of a "fifty–fifty" marriage is a recipe for endless strife. The traditional model based on sexual complementarity, on the other hand, is a 100–100 arrangement, in which both spouses fulfill their distinct roles to the best of their ability. Complementarity obviates conflict.

You cannot find out what people want by asking them, because their answers do not reflect the trade-offs necessary to get what they say they want. Many wives will answer "yes" if a feminist asks: "Would you like your husband to do half the housework?" But that only means they would like it *ceteris paribus*: if all other conditions were held constant. The feminist's inquiry should be: "Would you like your husband to turn down promotions and cut back on his working hours in order to do half the housework?" Wives do not commonly want to sacrifice any of their husband's income or professional prospects even if the gain in housework would be sufficient to get them featured in *Better Homes and Gardens*.

The demand schedule also explains why women will always have something to complain about. They complain "at the margin," as economists say, that they do not have the next item down on their demand schedule. They tacitly assume they should be able to get this item without giving up anything they already have. In other words, they have difficulty thinking in terms of trade-offs. An understanding of this may be of some comfort to harried husbands perplexed by their inability to make their wife happy.

Some women, for instance, are wont to complain that their work-obsessed husband does not pay enough attention to them. That does not mean their complaints would cease if he cut back on work and earnings to be with them more; it means only that they would switch to complaining about the material sacrifices that this change in behavior would necessitate. The husband in such a case must do what he knows is in his family's long-term best interest. He cannot permit an attention-seeking woman to come between him and his work in a vain attempt to remove all discontent from her life. Similarly, men are within their rights to tell their wife that keeping house is primarily a woman's responsibility: a husband is a provider and protector, not a butler.

On the other hand, there are also some misguided men today who press their wife to stay in the workforce because they do not like to have the second family income cut off. These men are not ideologically feminist; they just do not want to give up the extra vacations or fancy televisions that their wife's income makes possible. For reasons explained above, this is a devil's bargain; instead, men should be acting to shore up their own role.

12. WHAT IS TO BE DONE?

How, concretely, can men do that? I believe two policy goals are fundamental: one for the home and one for the workplace.

The linchpin of our family policy objectives must be the reestablishment of presumptive custody of children by their father. Women who wish to abandon their husband must forfeit their parental prerogatives and all claim to spousal support. That means dismantling the entire divorce industry. I have discussed these matters elsewhere.

Second, and in connection with the subject of the present essay, men must reestablish their rightful position in the world of work: I propose the slogan "Take Back the Day." This will require an end to antidiscrimination law as it relates to the sexes.

In part, the purpose of men's reestablishing themselves as breadwinners is simply to enable them to support children, of course. But it may also be necessary to make them attractive enough to women that they can *start* a family. We need to reestablish a "masculine mystique" in the mind of young women, teaching them once again that they are insufficient unto themselves and stand in need of a man. That is rarely obvious to a modern young woman with a well-paying job and no children. But plenty of evidence concerning fatherless homes indicates that men are as necessary to women as ever *over the course of a lifetime*. Men, too, need to understand that they have an essential role to play in the home—that the purposes of the family cannot be properly carried out in their absence.

A return to freedom of association, including the legalization of "discrimination," would benefit the world of work itself as well as home life. Men share thought and behavior patterns that permit more effective cooperation in an all-male setting than in mixed groups. And feminism has created a "hostile working environment" for men in most industries. Plenty of men would be eager to work for firms that formally barred women, far more than would presently be willing to say so out loud. Under a regime of free competition, all-male companies might quickly rout their "gender-equitable" competitors from the field. I suspect a lot of feminists are perfectly aware of this.

These recommendations are not primarily motivated by material considerations. I cannot guarantee the reader that implementing such proposals would raise the value of his stock portfolio. But my position is that the economy exists for the family and not the family for the economy. Family scholar Allan Carlson likes to note that during the postwar economic boom the traditional expression "childless marriage" began to be displaced by a new coinage: "child-free marriage." When a society values home entertainment systems more than children, something has gone terribly wrong.

The current mentality is not without historical precedent. Polybius notes the following of Hellenistic-era Boeotia:

> Childless men, when they died, did not leave their property to their nearest heirs, as had formerly been the custom there, but disposed of it for purposes of junketing and banqueting and made it the common property of their friends. Even many who had families distributed the greater part of their fortune among their clubs, so that there were many Boeotians who had more feasts to attend each month than there were days in it.

The wealth that corrupted ancient Boeotia would, of course, seem insupportable poverty to today's Americans.

Would Americans be able to accept a lower standard of living as a means to restoring the natural family? Probably not, but fortunately it does not matter what we can accept. Our long-postponed day of financial reckoning appears finally to be at hand, and it may well turn out to be something we should not wish away. When ordinary people are brought to understand that the state is unable to ensure their material well-being, children will again be perceived as long-term assets: necessary replacements for the Social Security swindle and state-seized or inflation-eroded private pension funds rather than obstacles to greater consumption. Amid the collapse of political finance, we may be able to regain a sense of the timeless *purpose* of labor and wealth. Our children may learn to find the satisfaction in the simple daily fact of family survival that we were unable to find in all our economic overreaching.

The Last Ditch, May–June, 2008

THE FAMILY WAY

Allan C. Carlson
Third Ways: How Bulgarian Greens, Swedish Housewives, And Beer-Swilling Englishmen Created Family-Centered Economies — And Why They Disappeared
Wilmington, Delaware: ISI Books, 2007

Economic science is so imposing an edifice viewed from outside — with its technical paraphernalia, its libraries full of books and journals, its endowed professorships and international conferences, its specialties and subspecialties — that the layman might be hesitant to take up the experts' time with questions about so petty a matter as a family. As Allan Carlson tells it, however, such deference to the economist's professional expertise would be misplaced: the natural family has remained a stumbling block to economic science as well as policymakers for more than two hundred years.

Adam Smith and David Ricardo expressed cautious optimism that an unhindered market in labor would provide the ordinary working man a large enough wage to marry and raise a few children; but neither claimed to have demonstrated the necessity for this. Radicals such as Marx and Engels soon challenged the idea, maintaining that capitalism transformed labor into an ordinary commodity which women and even children could sell to capitalists at a fraction of the cost for adult men. The traditional autonomy and solidarity of the family would thereby fall prey to industrial efficiency and the Faustian quest for profits. Later liberal economists such as J. S. Mill and Alfred Marshall came to agree with the Marxists that the capitalist market economy makes no natural accommodation to the family.

The Marxists also appear to be correct that the loss of family autonomy through wage competition is a development specific to capitalism. Alexander Chayanov, subject of one of Carlson's chapters, studied the preindustrial economy of peasant families and protested that the imposition of concepts like wages and capital on agrarian production was arbitrary and procrustean. The peasant family produced for use rather than profit; their work pattern was determined not by supply and demand but by natural biological rhythms: the recurrence of the seasons, sowing and reaping; the human life-cycle of birth, procreation and death. The analytic scheme of modern economics, which pre-supposes a fundamental distinction between capital and labor, is therefore of no help in elucidating what goes on in peasant households.

The "Third Ways" described in the present book were pro-grams designed to protect the natural family—peasant or oth-erwise—from the solvent of market competition. It consists of seven chapters of about twenty or thirty pages, each devoted to one "third way." They include programs to restore full-scale family farming, others just to promote home ownership and a modest degree of household production, and others still merely to guarantee a family-supporting wage to fathers.

It might at first sight seem paradoxical that families could ev-er be economically worse off having a second income instead of just one. But this is a classic example of what logicians call the fallacy of composition. It works like this. When an exciting play occurs in a baseball game, all the fans jump to their feet to get a better view. Do they actually get a better view? On average, no. If only one fan were to rise, *he* would get a better view; but when all rise, the overall view is no better than before. Analogously, an individual woman entering the workforce undoubtedly im-proves her own material situation; but if the great mass of wom-en enters the workforce, the overall effect is merely to glut the market for labor, driving down wages for everyone. As early as 1825, an editorial in a British newspaper declared:

> The labouring men of this country should return to the good old plan of subsisting their wives and children on the wages of their own labour and they should demand wages high enough for this purpose. By doing this, the capitalist will be obliged to give the same wages to men alone which they now give to men, women and children. [Labourers must] prevent their wives and children from

competing with them in the market and beating down the price of labour.

No "law of economics" prevents such insulation of women and children from the labor market. All societies treat certain things they especially value as *extra commerciam* — outside the scope of market exchange. There need be no market for beef, for example, in a country where cows are considered sacred. Or again, as long as a market in slaves existed they were subject to the same law of supply and demand as any other commodity; but this market could be abolished, and was. Similarly, there need be no market for women's labor in a country which values home life and family solidarity more than maximal industrial efficiency. Except under rare conditions involving extreme destitution — e.g., where women's or children's wage work might be necessary to allow everyone in a family to eat adequately — any society can enjoy as much family autonomy as it is willing to pay for in such efficiency. Proponents of family-centered "third ways" believe such a tradeoff worthwhile; some may disagree, but there is no economic absurdity involved in the idea.

If you are even familiar with the term "family wage" today, you are showing your age. Yet this ideal, writes Carlson, "dominated labor goals throughout the North Atlantic region from the mid-19th through mid-20th centuries and had measurable effects on wages and the labor market." While industrialists almost without exception advocated the "right" of poor women to work (and drive down men's wages), working class husbands felt differently. They fought for and won wages that permitted their women to remain at home with the children. In Britain between 1842 and 1914, for example, "substantial gains in material standards were achieved by the working class, accompanied by the movement of women from wage-earning to domestic pursuits." Similarly, in Belgium there was "a thorough transformation in the family life of workers between 1853 and 1891, based on a withdrawal of married women from the labor market and a dramatic rise in the real incomes of men." Keep this in mind the next time you hear a feminist complacently assert the "impossibility" of returning to the days when a woman's place was in the home.

In America the family wage ideal rested on legal barriers, direct discrimination against categories of female workers, marriage bans, and labor laws requiring the special treatment of women, discouraging their employment. The system was strong enough to survive the New Deal, but was dealt a body blow by the entry of the US into World War II and the consequent mobilization of women for industry. The National War Production Board recommended "a single evaluation line for all jobs in a plant regardless whether performed by men or women." Only 13% of US firms had followed such a policy in 1939, but by 1947, 57% did.

Carlson provides a graph of the erosion of the family wage system in America since 1951. Let the Family Wage Ratio be defined as the median income of dual earning couples divided by the median income of stay-at-home-wife couples. Under a family wage regime, this figure will approach 1.0; under the feminist gender-equivalence regime, the figure tends toward 2.0. In 1960, the figure was 1.25; it rose slowly in the '60s and '70s, and was still 1.42 as recently as 1982; then the rise accelerated, reaching 1.82 in 2003, the most recent date for which the book provides figures.

"Equal pay for equal work" is a masterful piece of political rhetoric with a sort of "2+2=4" ring to it. Carlson catalogues for us a few of the realities this deceptive slogan has served to conceal. First of all, family households with only a single male wage earner have experienced a *decline* in real income: between 1973 and 1993 alone, this decline amounted to 13.6%. Next, single-income families have been put at a mounting competitive disadvantage relative to two-income families in the acquisition of consumer goods. There has also been a sizeable increase in the number of men earning less than a "poverty line" wage, and similar growth in the number of children living in female-headed households. Married women are increasingly faced with a stark choice: leave their young children during the day to try to earn income, or stay with them and fall into poverty. Either way, the children lose.

For the first time in history, notes our author, the family is becoming completely industrialized. Gardening, food preparation, home repairs, child care, and other residual forms of home production are being abandoned by busy couples in favor of market-provided services; in other words, the home has no economy of its own, but has become at best a kind of consumer's cooperative. With the economic rationale for marriage thus eroded, divorce, transitory cohabitation, bastardy, abortion, and loneliness all increase. We have come a long way, baby.

Sweden is often held up as the best model of a country pursuing a "third way" between capitalism and socialism. Carlson devotes a chapter to the evolution of Swedish family policy in the past century and the ideological debates surrounding it; rumor has it that its original title was "Desperate Swedish Socialist Housewives." However that may be, this chapter makes especially clear the difficulty of arranging family policy prescriptions neatly on a conventional left-right ideological spectrum. As early as 1866, delegates to the First Socialist International "approved a resolution calling for bans on the employment of women. The measure's sponsors reasoned that working women pressed down overall wage levels and displaced men; in their view, working women were the equivalent of strikebreakers." Sweden's Social Democratic Party adopted this view, and for many years it remained normative for Swedish "progressives."

The author draws our attention, for instance, to Ellen Karolina Sofia Key: socialist, feminist, eugenics advocate, disciple of Darwin and Nietzsche. None of these commitments prevented her from laying heavy emphasis on the maternal role and its importance to individual women, their children and the society of the future. Woman was "most free," she wrote, "in the physical and psychic exercise of the function of maternity." The mother was an "artist in education" who understood "the enormous significance of the *first years*." What she most requires to fulfill this role properly is *time, time* and again *time*." She believed the State should place as high a priority upon proper mothering as upon military service. For many years a popular women's magazine, *Morning Breeze*, propagated Key's ideal of the socialist housewife, carrying illustrations of athletic-looking Nietzschean *Übermütter* surrounded by swarms of healthy children.

Gunnar and Alva Myrdals' pernicious influence on Swedish social politicy commenced in the 1930s, but was effectively resisted for longer than many realize. "Astonishingly," writes Carlson, "as late as 1964 the labor-force participation rate for Swedish women remained steady at 30 percent; a mere 3 percent of Swedish preschool children were in public daycare centers."

The socialist housewives began referring to homemaking as "domestic science" and portrayed themselves as efficient laborers whose work station just happened to be the home. They demanded and got several years of mandatory education in home economics and child care for all Swedish girls. Government agencies sponsored quantitative studies which revealed, *inter alia*, that the average working-class housewife had at her disposal 2.8 frying pans and 1.6 teapots. The modern Swedish household was clearly a highly scientific place.

By the 1960s, however, Alva Myrdal and her stridently anti-familial feminism were again on the march. Individual rather than familial taxation became a central issue in Swedish politics. As passage of the measure approached, a "Campaign for the Family" was launched. Fifty thousand letters of protest poured into the Prime Minister's office; thousands of women marched on the Riksdag in (as one Swedish newspaper put it) "history's first housewife demonstration."

It was to no avail. In 1970, individual taxation went into effect; overnight, a housewife became an expensive luxury. Carlson writes: "Correctly labeled the era of Red Sweden, the first Olaf Palme government committed a kind of feminist genocide, intentionally eliminating a whole class of women through coerced 'reeducation' and forced labor."

The family wage is by nature a compromise with industrial capitalism; it turns one member of the family over to the labor market in exchange for keeping the rest insulated from it. Distributism, the economic platform advocated by Hilaire Belloc and G. K. Chesterton, went farther by seeking to counteract some of the inherent tendencies of capitalism directly.

The Distributists believed property "so important that every family should have some." But capitalism, they asserted, naturally brought about the consolidation of property in a few hands.

The state, therefore, should openly favor smallholders, cooperatives and family businesses over large corporations and monopolies. They advocated progressive taxation and legal restrictions on large enterprises. In his chapter on the Distributist movement, Carlson is in the odd position of having to defend Chesterton in particular from some of his greatest admirers, too quick to dismiss this aspect of his work as incoherent, vacuous, or futile. Such is the usual price of political failure.

For a similar economic program that made real headway, Carlson turns our attention to the peasant parties which swept to power in the new democracies of Eastern Europe after the Great War. Their fundamental principle was that land should belong to those who till it. This required extensive land redistribution from the old nobility to peasant families, sometimes without compensation. In Czechoslovakia, 4.5 million acres were distributed to peasant families by 1931; in Poland the figure was 6.25 million acres by 1937.

The peasant parties also favored progressive taxation, free trade, republicanism, decentralized governance, agricultural cooperatives, pacifism, educational reform, mandatory public service for youth, rural life, and *limited* industrialization (the processing of agricultural and forest products, for instance, being preferable to machine gun or mustard gas production). The peasant parties also uniformly opposed communism. A "Green International," formally called the International Agrarian Bureau, took form in 1923 to coordinate political action across international boundaries. One specific project aimed at creating a Danubian free trade zone in Central and Eastern Europe.

A fluke of history allowed agrarian ideas to influence policy even in the Soviet Union for a time. In 1921 Lenin announced the New Economic Policy, a tactical retreat on the economic front aimed at allowing the Bolsheviks to tighten their political grip on Russia. For most of the 1920s, collectivization of peasant landholdings was shelved and private industry on a modest scale was permitted. The agrarian economist Alexander Chayanov openly directed an agrarian think tank in Moscow from 1919 until 1930, and even became Deputy Minister of Agriculture for a time.

Despite their promising beginnings, all these agrarian programs succumbed to more ruthless enemies of various sorts. Peasant rule was violently overthrown in Bulgaria in 1923; then in Poland in 1926. The new Yugoslav government gradually squelched it in Croatia during the '20s, and in Romania it lost out to royalist militarism by 1930. Stalin had Chayanov arrested and sent to the Gulag that same year. A number of peasant leaders ended by being assassinated. In Czechoslovakia, however, peasant rule continued all the way up to the Nazi occupation.

Anyone familiar with the "Christian Democratic" parties of contemporary Europe will be suspicious of their inclusion in a volume devoted to "third way" politics. Carlson recognizes this; he explains that in the course of the 1950s these parties either faded from the scene (as in France) or

> consolidated their hold on power at the price of their vision. By the early 1960s, they were increasingly pragmatic and bureaucratic, self-satisfied defenders of the status quo. Ambitious office seekers rather than Christian idealists came to dominate the parties. [They] became simply mass parties of the right-of-center.

If you want to understand what is wrong with the Old Continent today, study the Christian Democrats of Germany or Italy.

Yet Christian Democracy has distinguished roots extending back into the 19th century. Its progenitors were believers who abhorred the anti-Christian aspects of the French Revolution but had no particular concern for the preservation of monarchy, feudal titles or great private fortunes. They rejected liberal individualism and laid emphasis on the family as a natural institution which the State was bound to protect and defend.

Many sought to unify Christians of various denominations politically in order to counteract the secularizing tendency of the modern world. Abraham Kuyper, for example, was a Protestant clergyman who helped found the Antirevolutionary Party of the Netherlands; he saw Catholics as natural allies in the struggle against Christendom's enemies. Kuyper's influence on American Evangelicals has been extensive, but remains little known outside Evangelical circles.

German Catholics were also among the early founders of Christian Democracy. Bishop Ketteler of Mainz helped organize "The Catholic Federation of Germany" in 1848, which was later renamed the Center Party and opened to Protestants. "During the 1860s," writes Carlson, "Ketteler denounced 'capitalist absolutism,' called for the creation of Christian labor associations to protect workers, and urged political reforms that would increase wages, shorten the working day, and prohibit the labor of children and mothers in factories." He was also a principle opponent of Bismarck's so-called *Kulturkampf* of the 1870s. This campaign succeeded in abolishing church weddings and forbidding the discussion of political matters from the pulpit. Until he met opposition, Bismarck also attempted to give the State a large degree of control over clerical affairs.

Leo XIII's encyclical *Rerum Novarum* had great influence on Catholic Christian Democratic thinkers (as well as on the Distributists). Although often misunderstood as merely a rejection of socialism, the document "implicitly declared over 80 percent of Europe's land—circa 1891—to be held unjustly. In effect, [it was] a call for peaceful agrarian revolution." The document became a part of the Center Party's platform.

Hitler abolished the Center Party in 1933; Mussolini had already outlawed its Italian Christian Democratic counterpart in 1925. During the years it was forced out of public life, the Christian Democratic tradition was carried on at a philosophical level by a number of French Catholics: Emmanuel Mounier, his student Gilbert Dru (murdered by the Gestapo), Etienne Gilson, Etienne Borne, and Jacques Maritain. To the liberal individualism which spoke of the self as a locus of desires they opposed "personalism," which stressed moral choice and the development of the personality through participation in social bodies such as the family and local community. They held that women should enjoy equal civil, legal, and political rights, but believed this compatible with the family wage ideal and traditional sex roles.

Christian Democratic parties had a decisive influence on the politics of the immediate postwar period, coming to power in

West Germany and Italy while taking part in governing coalitions in France and the Netherlands. The UN Universal Declaration of Human Rights has been described as "largely identical" with the worldview of Christian Democracy, and the original European Economic Community was also their work.

The most important economic thinker associated with the original Christian Democratic movement was Wilhelm Röpke. Although he was the mind behind the West German *Wirtschaftswunder* of the 1950s (through his influence on Economic Minister Ludwig Erhard), Röpke was the first to criticize the "cult of productivity" as a "disorder of spiritual perception." Insisting that "people do not live by cheap vacuum cleaners alone," he sought "to adapt economic policy to man, not man to economic policy."

While defending private property and free markets, Röpke insisted that a successful market economy required a moral framework—one which was not itself a product of market relations, but of "family, church, genuine communities, and tradition." Like the Distributists, he favored regulatory measures to prevent monopolies and encourage home ownership, small-shops, and family farms.

None of the third ways the author describes proved a complete success; but none was without positive effects, and often more than commonly realized. More importantly, the problems to which third way advocates responded are with us still: the collapse of Communism does not imply that the West has succeeded in reconciling the family's needs with the demands of a competitive industrial economy.

The Occidental Quarterly, vol. 8, no. 3 (Fall 2008): 99–108

Back to Africa:
Sexual Atavism
in the Modern West *

About the middle of the "roaring twenties," as America was enjoying a spell of peace and prosperity, the eminent literary critic Irving Babbitt issued a dire warning:

> Sexual unrestraint [he wrote] is wreaking fearful havoc to society. . . . The resultant diseases are . . . a menace to the future of the white race. . . . There is an undoubted connection between a certain type of . . . self-indulgent individualism and an unduly declining birthrate. The French and also the Americans of native descent are, if we are to trust statistics, in danger of withering from the earth. Where the population is increasing, it is, we are told, at the expense of quality. The stocks to which the past has looked for its leaders are dying out and the inferior or even degenerate breeds are multiplying.

When Babbitt came to consider possible ways of remedying the situation, however, he acknowledged: "the evidence is slight that the individual can be induced to control himself on such general grounds as the good of the country or . . . the good of the white race menaced by 'the rising tide of color.'" He goes on to argue that traditional ideals of self restraint would be of greater practical effect than explicitly eugenic considerations. One might add that external constraints are sometimes more effective than either, and that it was in fact the discipline imposed by the Great Depression and Second World War which actually put an end to the profligacy (sexual and otherwise) of the twenties. These hardships were followed, not accidentally, by the baby boom.

---

* I would like to thank Steve Sailer, Henry Harpending, and Peter Frost for directing me to some relevant anthropological literature. The views expressed are my own.

But the baby boom turned out to be a kind of one generation wonder. Today the sexual situation in the Western world has reverted to a condition worse than Babbitt could have imagined possible, and his warnings are timelier than when he gave them.

And I want particularly to reiterate his point that racial purposes are not necessarily best achieved by adducing explicitly racial considerations. While it is important to publicize accurate information about race, we cannot continue our civilization simply by winning debates about IQ scores. Ideas may have consequences, but they do not have children. And normal people do not make basic life decisions involving marriage and children on the basis of scientific findings or considerations of racial politics.

I would even caution against too heavy an emphasis on the issue of intermarriage. Whites actually seem to marry outside their race less often than others: Sam Francis called the numbers "negligible." On the other hand, vast numbers of our women are either not reproducing or doing so at below replacement level. Yet some racialists seem to be more concerned over one interracial union than fifty childless white couples. The reason, I believe, is that they can *see* the occasional white mother pushing her mulatto baby around in a stroller, but they cannot see the white children other women are *not* having. The greatest threats to a nation, however, need not be those which strike the eye.

Today I want to share with you some thoughts on the dire threat posed to our race and civilization by a movement to which some racialists may not attend because it seems to be non-racial in character: sexual liberation. In my essay "Sexual Utopia in Power," I explained why a polygamous mating pattern inevitably emerges with the breakdown of marriage. This is *not* because evil men are able to exploit helpless, innocent lasses; it is simply the natural result of women's own socially unconstrained choices. They themselves compete to mate with the most attractive males, in a manner we can directly observe among the lower mammals. Now, even among humans, polygamous societies are nothing new, and a great deal is known about how they operate. It so happens that the most polygamous part of the world is a region of special interest to Americans—it is none other than West Africa, the ancestral homeland of our own black population. A look at that society might shed some useful light on what is happening in the West today.

An unusual feature of the region is that women produce nearly all the food: one anthropologist calls it "the region of female farming *par excellence.*" This is not because Africans have an enlightened and progressive belief in careers for women, but because West African agriculture is of an unusually primitive type. Cultivation tends to be extensive rather than intensive, and the principle tools are simple hoes which women can wield as easily as men. The more challenging climate of Europe, by contrast, calls for intensive plough cultivation, entailing female dependence on male provisioning.

Since the women of West Africa can provide for themselves, and often for their husbands as well, men do not need to worry about the cost of taking multiple wives. A wife may even, contrary to our expectations, take the initiative to encourage her husband to marry another woman, since this usually relieves her of some of her chores. As for the men—well, they end up enjoying considerable leisure, which they mostly devote to politicking, fighting, drinking and the pursuit of what ethnographers delicately refer to as "polycoity." A Dutch traveler left us an amusing description of the typical polygamist on the 17th-century Gold Coast, who "idly spends his time in impertinent tattling and drinking of palm-wine, which the poor wives are frequently obliged to raise money to pay for." Husbands are not even duty-bound to share any personal earnings with their wives; community of property is not assumed to be part of the definition of marriage.

Moreover, polygamous husbands are positively discouraged from spending too much time or becoming too emotionally intimate with any particular wife, as this would tend to provoke jealousy in the rest and thus interfere with the smooth functioning of the household. Most wives, therefore, are resigned to marital neglect. On the other hand, in a polygamous society there will always be plenty of footloose bachelors roaming about who are more than willing to keep lonely harem-wives company. Few of these African women are Roman Lucretias prepared to plunge daggers into their breasts to preserve their sacred honor. In fact, sometimes the whole distinction between licit and illicit relations becomes blurred, and men and women lose any notion of a permanent marriage bond. They simply have "relationships." (Is this starting to sound familiar?) The upshot of the whole mess is that paternity in West Africa tends to be extremely uncertain. As a result, men do not put much effort into fatherhood; why should they when they do not even know whether the children are theirs?

The weakness of fatherhood in Africa makes for an emphasis on kinship through the maternal line; anthropologists describe African family life as "matrifocal." But this does not mean that mothers make up for the neglect of children by fathers. They are often content to delegate care of their offspring to more distant relatives or friends to whom they pay a modest fee. This practice, known as "fosterage," is in no way seen as a dereliction of a mother's duties in black Africa. Why do mothers do it? One motive is that the absence of children from the house may make them more attractive to new male suitors. Fosterage can begin when the child is quite young, since early weaning allows the mother's ovulation cycle to recommence quickly. Relieved of her offspring, she is able to devote her full attention to having more babies. In other words, the effort she saves on childrearing goes into child*bearing*. The obvious result is a vast number of lackadaisically reared children. (It is perhaps worth mentioning that, in another parallel with the "progressive" West, Africans do not bother to raise boys and girls very differently, though such "nonsexist" upbringing has not led to any egalitarian paradise there either.)

Western humanitarians appalled by what seems to them the scandalous poverty of Africa and anxious to relieve it are sometimes surprised to learn that Africans themselves do not share their concerns. They seem breezily confident the children will get along somehow. This may be a racial trait, but it is undoubtedly reinforced by the practice of fosterage: parents who delegate care of their children to others do not feel the same need to husband their own resources carefully. Once the children are out of the house, they may have little idea what kind of care they are actually getting. Clearly, this is an invitation to wishful thinking.

Finally, as the number of children in fosterage grows, the small fees paid out to the foster parents begin to add up. The biological parents' money is bled off, and capital is not accumulated. Even relatively prosperous families usually have no "nest egg" in our sense. This is an important factor contributing to the poverty of the region.

In summary, we may describe this whole family system as based on short-term responses to circumstances rather than deliberate, long-term planning.

Now, the simpler and more spontaneous culture of West Africa may more or less be able to muddle along in this fashion, but the civilization which produced Shakespeare, Mozart, and Newton cannot. The achievements which form our cultural heritage presuppose stable social arrangements. Predictable familial and civic relations, long apprenticeships, capital accumulation, and the rational allocation of resources are what allow men of talent to invest time and effort in endeavors which do not necessarily have any quick or obvious economic payoff. This is what makes the arts and sciences possible.

It is probably true that Europeans are naturally better adapted (through evolutionary pressures) to monogamy and deferral of gratification, but it would behoove us not to presume too much upon this. One of the reasons for studying Africa is that it is like a window onto our own remotest past. During declining phases of civilization, primitive cultural forms tend to reappear. Whites are not immune to what might be called "re-Africanization," and there is plentiful evidence that some such thing is now taking place. Western man is in certain ways returning spiritually to the Dark Continent from which he laboriously emerged long ago.

In the first place, let us consider the contemporary West's obvious and abnormal preoccupation with sex. Anthropologists speak of reproductive effort as a combination of mating effort and parenting effort. There is a natural tradeoff between these two components. The less time people spend looking for mates, the more they have left to devote to their children. The traditional European practice is to encourage young people to pair off early and emphasize fidelity in order to reduce sexual competition and allow adults to concentrate on the serious business of raising families.

But this is not a universal human pattern. Africans make the tradeoff between mating effort and parenting effort differently, with the result that sex assumes greater importance in their lives over a longer period of time. White writers of earlier days frequently noted the prominence of sex in the black man's thoughts; when recalled now, such observations are, of course, cited with horror as proof of our ancestor's terrible "racism." In fact they were merely reporting what they observed, and what is still observed by professional anthropologists in West Africa today.

As monogamy continues to decay in the West, our mating system increasingly comes to resemble the more competitive African model, and with similar results. We see young women become completely consumed by the effort to maximizing their sexual allure in order to snag high status men, and men competing for status in order to obtain access to these women. All this comes at the expense of childrearing and family life.

Secondly, the feminist program of cajoling or forcing women into the workplace means that women once again become self-supporting, as are the female farmers of West Africa. The *Dilbert* world of air-conditioned work cubicles may not outwardly resemble the miserable farming plots of Africa. But both stand in marked contrast to the male-breadwinner model traditional in the West, in which devoted childrearing was a woman's first and most important duty. Indeed, the modern workplace, optimized for risk-free, repetitious, sedentary work is probably the best conceivable environment for eliminating women's economic dependence upon men. By the same token, it discourages the moderately large families of well-brought-up children which are the indispensable and timeless precondition of Western Civilization. If sufficiently many women fail or refuse to marry and become mothers of such families, our way of life cannot be sustained.

The most important effect of economic autonomy upon women is that it reduces the benefits of monogamous marriage to them. This affords them the freedom to mate as they please, which naturally results in catty competition over the most attractive men. That is what the college "hook-up" scene is really about (and not callous men "preying upon" wide-eyed virgins). The women use attractive men partly for pleasure, but often just as much to demonstrate their sexual powers to other women; they use affluent men for their resources (either not marrying or marrying and then divorcing them), and they rely on the police to get rid of "stalkers and harassers," i.e., men who find them attractive but for whom they have no use.

A second economic factor influencing female sexual behavior today is easy consumer credit. The credit card functions similarly to the expectation of providing for children through fosterage in Africa. It conceals from young, present-centered women the need for frugality. The contemporary American economy is fueled to a great extent by massive consumer debt. How much of this reckless spending do you suppose is done by married men with children to support? Feminists complain that men continue to earn more than women, but they say little about which sex *spends* more. And, of course, the more time and effort women devote to careers and personal consumption, the less they have for such children as they do manage to bear. The phenomenon of "latchkey children," raised by television sets and unsupervised peer groups, was an entirely predictable result of the feminist project.

So, in summary: the contemporary West resembles traditional West African society in (1) female economic self-support; (2) polygamous and unstable mating patterns; (3) absence of long range planning or deferred gratification; (4) a tendency to overestimate available resources; and (5) low investment parenting.

But all analogies break down at some point, and when this one does it is to the credit of Africa rather than us. The African system does not, as I noted, produce a particularly advanced civilization, but it does at least ensure procreation, which is more than can be said for our present way of life. Although Africans do not usually sacrifice all that much for their offspring, they *are* extremely fond of children. They have a proverb: "If you have a child, you have a life." One of the justifications they offer for practicing fosterage is that without it the poor foster-parent would be deprived of the pleasure of juvenile company. Africans not only want to have children, they want to share them with all their friends and neighbors. Accordingly, efforts by Western busybodies to interest them in birth control have not met with much success: fourteen of the sixteen most fertile countries in the world are in black Africa.

Sociobiologists speak of high investment vs. high fertility reproductive strategies, but it is clear the contemporary West does not fall into either category. We are practicing both low fertility and low parental investment. It is uncanny how many of the "progressive" causes being pushed among us involve thwarting procreation: female careerism, unrestricted abortion, so-called "safe sex," and special political protections for homosexuality. A society which makes these its priorities can only have a death wish.

Much has already been written in the conservative press in condemnation of the sexual revolution, of course, but in my view most of the criticism is worse than worthless because it is simply an expression of male rescue fantasies rather than an informed and rational assessment of the situation. Thus, there are calls for greater protection for women whose chief problem is that they are overprotected to begin with. Lonely bachelors who could easily find a wife in a monogamous society are portrayed as dangerous predators upon female innocence when the only reason they remain bachelors is that women are furiously competing to join the harems of a few unusually handsome and successful men. Hard working men are berated for failing to provide for women who enjoy preferences in hiring and advancement at their expense and have better economic prospects than they do.

The misguided gallantry of the typical male pundit may to some extent simply be a component of male heterosexuality: since men naturally desire women, they have a vested interest in believing women worth having. Conservatives who cannot heap enough ridicule upon Rousseau's doctrine of the natural goodness of man are often among the most naïve in asserting the natural goodness of woman. This is a kind of ideology, with an ide-

ology's characteristic capacity to ignore or explain away conflict-
ing evidence. Many men continue to insist, in defiance of all the
evidence of women's actual behavior, that they are pining away
for morally upright men to love, honor, and obey, and that the
poor dears cannot find happiness only because other men (never
the writer himself, of course) are selfish, irresponsible cads.

To some extent, I sympathize with these commentators. It is
indeed baffling that any woman could prefer the barren existence of the career woman to having a home with a devoted husband and offspring to care for. I once heard a man observe that if
young women had any sense they would be in the streets de-
manding the return of the meal ticket that marriage once gave
them. But actions speak louder than words, and obviously this is
not happening. The short term incentives of independent incomes, material self-indulgence, and transitory "relationships"
with attractive men are visibly winning out over the long term
benefits to women of marriage and family. It is past time for
men to wake up to this reality.

The most important form of "racial activism" is childrearing.
This goal cannot be achieved by the conservative's usual ham-
fisted methods of calling for more punishment of men, making
endless excuses for women, and putting everyone to sleep with
moral exhortation about the sacredness of marriage. Instead, we
must consider the actual incentives now operating upon men
and women, as economists long ago learned to do, and focus our
efforts on altering them in ways conducive to family formation.

Let me illustrate what I mean with reference to the issue of
racial intermarriage, which as I said some racialists counterpro-
ductively harp upon. Today there are more than a few American
men going to enormous trouble and expense to seek wives in
exotic places like the Philippine Islands and South America. For
the most part, they are doing so not because they lust after exotic
flesh but because the women in these societies treat men better,
are more feminine, and give family life priority over any work
they may do outside the home. It is futile to say to such men,
"You have a racial duty to beg a spoiled Western girl to accept a
diamond ring from you and put up with her nagging until such
time as she gets bored, walks off with the children, and sues you

for child support." White men do not have any such duty, and outside the ranks of a few hardcore racialists, such exhortations will be entirely without effect. If you wish to influence the average man of the West, who does not read *American Renaissance* or *The Occidental Quarterly* or perhaps even think much about race directly, to marry a white woman and start a family as his ancestors did, the only way to do it is to make white women marriageable once again. This means undoing at least forty years of feminism.

Or again, let us consider those white women who take up with black men. This too is happening for a reason. There has been plenty written about the injustices of so-called affirmative action, even by mainstream conservatives, but I have never anywhere seen a direct discussion of its sexual consequences. Given the hypergamous nature of the female sex instinct, however, there certainly are such consequences. Our current laws mean that white men are in effect being forced to labor for the benefit of blacks. Furthermore, they must carefully watch their words to avoid "offending" blacks, but not vice-versa. Women perceive all this: they have a keen sense of which males are dominant. Once again, direct attempts to change behavior through scolding and exhortation are simply not likely to be effective. It is the incentives to which these women are responding which must be changed.

Far from women being naturally monogamous, as our fathers were often encouraged to believe, the family probably first came into being when men forcibly imposed monogamy upon women in order to insure their own paternity and minimize sexual competition. But, once established, the benefits of the system were so great that women came to appreciate it as well. If our civilization is to survive, we must join together again to restore the monogamous heterosexual family as the normal unit of society.

A much-shortened version of this article was published in *American Renaissance*, vol. 19, no. 6, June 2008

THE QUESTION OF FEMALE MASOCHISM

"If He Doesn't Hit You, He Doesn't Love You." So runs an African proverb. Or a Russian proverb, according to other sources. Or a Bolivian proverb, according to still others. Perhaps it is all three. A similar Latin American saying, "The more you hit me, the more I love you," turns up over 100,000 results on Google.

It is hardly a new idea that female sexuality has a masochistic component. Indeed, this seems to be part of the folk wisdom of the world; in other words, it corresponds the observations of many persons of both sexes across many generations. Yet it is not easy to find extended discussion of it. Within the past century, most writing on the subject has been beholden to the Freudian tradition, a circumstance that does not inspire confidence. A more hopeful sign may be the sizable feminist literature aimed at refuting "the *myth* of female masochism." If nothing else, such literature is testimony to the enduring reality of the corresponding folk belief; no one writes polemics against things that have absolutely no basis in reality.

It is not hard to understand why persons of both sexes are reluctant to talk about female masochism. No one wants to appear to be condoning the abuse of women. A prime component of masculinity is the instinct to *protect* women. In the European tradition, this has given rise to the principle that "a gentlemen never strikes a lady." Pushing gallantry to the point of silliness, as usual, Thomas Fleming writes in *Chronicles* that "there is something unmanly about beating women, unmanly and sickening."

But what if there is something in at least some women that responds positively to male violence? The British anti-feminist "Angry Harry" shares this anecdote:

> Emma Humphreys (a *cause célèbre* for feminists in the UK) had served some time in prison for killing her boy-

friend. But, following vociferous claims from various wimmin's groups that she had acted in self-defense against his violence, she was released.

When she was interviewed by the BBC on Radio 4 she had been out of prison only for ten days. And yet she admitted that she was already in another abusive relationship with a man who "slapped her about" frequently.

Further, she stated that love and abuse were part and parcel of each other, and that you couldn't have one without the other. *"If he doesn't hit you then he doesn't love you."* [my emphasis]

The interview was cut short at this point with a very embarrassed female interviewer having to cover for the missing time.

Another example: Hollywood earns its profits by appealing to the fantasies of its audience, including women; if the product fails to strike the audience's imagination, it flops. Some lessons about what female audiences like can be drawn from the early career of Clark Gable. The film that made him a star was *A Free Soul* (1931), in which he played a gangster who pushes Norma Shearer around to let her know who's boss.

As a fan site puts it, previous male leads had been "suave and svelte, romantic and tender." Gable's character:

> was supposed to be the villain, the evil corrupt criminal that you are supposed to root against—it's Leslie Howard you are supposed to hope Norma ends up with—plain vanilla Leslie Howard. Well, the fans spoke and spoke loudly—the 1931 woman didn't want plain vanilla and no longer wanted "powder puff" men with styled hair and ruffles on their shirts—they wanted a real man, a rough man, a man who was a bit dirty and not afraid to put them in their place.[1]

Gable followed up this role with that of a sinister chauffeur

---

[1] http://dearmrgable.com/?p=4970

who knocks Barbara Stanwyck out cold with one punch in *Night Nurse*. These were the last supporting roles he was ever to play. Bushels of fan mail began arriving at the studio. Some breathless women are said to have offered to let Gable hit them!

Or consider this real-life Hollywood story, quoted by Steven E. Rhoads in his valuable book *Taking Sex Differences Seriously* (New York: Encounter Books, 2005):

> Eddy Fisher and Debbie Reynolds both tell of a dinner party at their house where Mike Todd and Elizabeth Taylor started belting each other. Todd ended up dragging Taylor across the floor by her hair as she kicked and scratched. When Reynolds became alarmed and jumped on Todd's back to get him to stop, Todd and Taylor both turned on her. According to Fisher, Taylor said, "Oh Debbie . . . Don't be such a Girl Scout. Really, Debbie, you're so square."

Todd and Taylor were fighting *in order to* "make up" afterwards. It is not uncommon for wives to provoke their husbands into hitting them for precisely this reason.

Many of the "battered women" we are encouraged to sympathize with have a remarkable tendency to suffer from abuse at the hands of *every* man with whom they become involved. Tammy Wynette, the Country singer who gained fame with the song "Stand By Your Man," was married to five men and left four of them (managing to die with her fifth marriage still intact). Most of her husbands are said to have abused her in some way, and teary-eyed retellings of her "tragic" life have been offered to the public.

I remind the reader of the central principle of male-female relations: *women choose*. They represent the supply; men represent the demand. If Tammy Wynette never took up with a man who failed to abuse her, there can be only one explanation: *Tammy had a thing for nasty boys*.

If you put a woman like this in a room with a dozen men, within five minutes she would be exclusively focused on the meanest, most domineering and brutal fellow in the room. Some women who had alcoholic fathers have a similar uncanny ability to detect the alcoholic in a room full of men, even if he is sober at the moment. "Women's intuition" is a reality: it is an ability to pick up on tiny signals, slight nuances of facial expression that would go unnoticed by a man.

We are attracted to qualities in the opposite sex which our own sex lacks. For many women, this means an attraction to male brutality. Such women may claim to want a sensitive fellow who is in touch with his feelings, but this bears no relation to their behavior. What women say about men comes from their cerebral cortex; how they choose men depends upon their evolutionary more primitive limbic system. Even campus feminists choose arrogant jocks to "hook up" with, not male feminists in touch with their emotions. I have heard it suggested that the best reason not to strike a woman today is that you will never be able to get rid of her afterwards.

Why don't such women simply *tell* their men that they find violence and dominance exciting? Perhaps it would destroy the fantasy to say "I'm in the mood, so could you please slap me around for a bit?" In most cases, the women are probably just behaving instinctively, not understanding their own motivations. In any case, it would obviously be useful for well-intentioned husbands to *understand* this aspect of women's sexuality. It might prevent more serious violence and even save a few marriages.

The very first thing contemporary dating gurus teach men is not to be a "nice guy." Nor is this aversion to "niceness" exclusive to feminine psychology: even men understand the pejorative connotations of the word *innocuous*.

Perhaps more important than piling up more examples to attest the phenomenon is giving a little thought to *why* female masochism occurs. Like other sex traits, it is an evolutionary adaptation. I am going to go way out on a limb and suggest that early hominid males may not have been quite so delicate as Tom Fleming, who becomes ill at the very thought of a woman being struck. African men are, by all accounts, pretty quick with their fists to this day. Gallantry is an achievement of civilization, not a part of our primitive nature.

Now, females in our "environment of evolutionary adaptation" were dependent on males for mating, protection, and access to resources. These males were bigger and stronger than females and could easily hurt them if angered or displeased. If our female ancestors had been delicate snowflakes unable to endure life with such brutes, we would not be here today. In other words, women *adapted* to male brutality, including occasional violence, learning how to get through or around it.

Think for a moment, men, how *you* would learn to behave if you were dependent for survival on an unpredictable and often violent creature larger and stronger than yourself. You would learn not simply to take what you wanted. You would learn to act when his back is turned, to use indirection, deception, manipulation. You would learn to conceal your true thoughts and keep Big Boy confused as to your true intentions. You would, in short, learn to act like a woman.

The battle of the sexes is a contest of force vs. cunning. Yes, civilized men learn to control their aggressive impulses and not beat women up every time they feel irritation with them. In the modern West, men have largely renounced the use of their natural weapon for controlling women, i.e., force. Have women renounced the use of their own weapons against men? Certainly we cannot expect women to shed millennial evolutionary adaptations automatically the instant men learn to behave.

Women's basic strategy during courtship is still to keep suitors confused. Their primary method of getting what they want is still the indirect route through influencing their men. When they express aggression, it still usually takes the form of passive aggression. And they are still both more frequent and more effective liars than men.

To judge by self-help literature aimed at women, most conceive the task of finding a mate as one of figuring out "how to flatter, tease, dupe, and otherwise manipulate a man into marriage" (Rhoads, p. 120). Does it never occur to women that if they *really were* loyal, sincere, and feminine, men might not *need* to be duped into marrying them?

While I am not holding my breath for feminism to demand an end to feminine wiles, I think it possible for women to overcome the uglier side of their nature just as men learn to control their temper and instinct for aggression. Women who relied on trickery and deception in their dealings with the opposite sex used to be referred to pejoratively as "designing women"—an expression which has largely disappeared from our language.

In short, I would be more inclined to sympathize with all the campaigns opposing "violence against women" if they were coupled with their logical counterpart: opposing "fraud against men."

Another interesting aspect of campaigns against domestic abuse to consider is: Why now? Are men behaving more violently today than they used to? There seems to be no evidence for this. As early as 2000, Massachusetts District Court Judge Milton H. Raphaelson declared that there exists "not an epidemic of domestic violence, but an epidemic of hysteria about domestic violence." Insofar as there is any real problem of women being brutalized in Western countries, it mainly involves recent non-Western immigrant populations, a fact systematically ignored or concealed by feminists.

Popular concerns are often weirdly unrelated to actual circumstances. It was only in the 1960s, after the percentage of Americans failing to complete secondary school had been falling for decades and had reached an historic low, that Americans discovered the problem of "high school dropouts."

Political and economic conditions in France steadily improved in the decades leading up to the French Revolution; as Tocqueville explained, expectations rose faster than conditions could improve, so more humane government was accompanied by growing dissatisfaction over "despotism." A similar process may underlie contemporary hysteria over "intimate partner violence."

Many have commented on the "irony" that the most pampered women in history are the ones complaining most about oppression. Perhaps we should consider whether this does not represent an irony but a direct causal relation: whether modern woman complains of her lot because—rather than in spite of—its being so favorable.

Jack Donovan has made an ethological argument in favor of

such an interpretation.[2] Bonobos, or pygmy chimpanzees, are physically not very different from other chimps, but they are now classed as a separate species because of radical differences in their behavior. Bonobo males are not very aggressive. They compete less for status than do male chimps, and they do not compete at all for mates. Sex is promiscuous, and males are not possessive. Homosexual mating is common. All parenting is done by mothers. Female bonds are stronger and more enduring than male bonds. In short, bonobo society is a feminist paradise.

Chimpanzee behavior is the opposite of bonobo behavior in almost every respect. Male chimps form hierarchical gangs and compete constantly for status and access to females. They are violent and territorial, forming alliances both to defend their own territory and raid that of other chimpanzee bands. They kill stray males from other bands when the opportunity presents itself. They push females around, and females are expected to display submission to males. Homosexuality is uncommon among them. Chimpanzee social behavior is a feminist's worst nightmare.

Evolutionary theory would lead us to look for a difference in the living environments of bonobos and chimps to which their radically different behavior could represent adaptations. And the primatologists have found such a difference: chimps must compete with other species, especially gorillas, for food. The bonobos live in a food-rich, gorilla-free environment where the living is easy. It is this lack of competitors which makes violence, hierarchy, competition, and male bonding unnecessary for bonobos.

Western man is like a chimp who has done his job too well. Having defeated nearly all his dangerous competitors, he finds himself without much of a function in a prosperous society that no longer needs to be defended. It is only to be expected that his women are going to start bitching that he needs to learn to act more like a bonobo. Feminism is a byproduct of peace and prosperity, not a response to patriarchy and oppression.

---

[2] Jack Donovan, *The Way of Men* (Milwaukee, Or.: Dissonant Hum, 2012), "The Bonobo Masturbation Society."

Some contemporary female behavior, such as that catalogued by Michelle Langley, seems more akin to sadism than to masochism (see chapter 2, above). But this does not necessarily contradict what we have written: sadism is merely the opposite face of masochism. I would suggest that female sadism might be expected to emerge in a society where men refuse to or are prevented from displaying dominance. A society-wide failure of men to take charge of women is likely to produce a great deal of conscious or unconscious sexual frustration in women which may express itself as sadism.

Is the Violence Against Women Act an attempt to get back at men for their failure to put women in their place? Surely women would rather have Clark Gable than take out more restraining orders, force men to take more anger management classes, enjoy more absurd police-state protections from men who are increasingly wimpy anyway.

I do not know if frustrated masochistic instincts cause sadism in women—it is just my hunch. What I do feel confident in stating is that female masochism is a critically important subject which neither feminist denial nor the sanctimonious gallantry of Christian traditionalists should dissuade us from investigating.

Counter-Currents/*North American New Right*
September 17, 2014

Epilogue:
Writing & Responding to
the Present Book

I started to develop the views presented in the following essays around the year 2000, based initially on the surprising things I was starting to find in obscure corners of the internet — what later became known as the "manosphere," then in its infancy. For a long time, most of my waking hours were devoted to thinking through what I was learning, tracing it back to first principles and forward to its ramifications in different domains. It was intellectually exciting to discover a whole new way of thinking about relations between the sexes; at the same time, much of it was heartbreaking to an old romantic such as I used to be.

Toward the end of 2005, throwing caution to the wind, I tried to get down as much of my new thought as I could in a single essay. The result was "Sexual Utopia in Power," the title being a combination of *Utopia in Power*, Heller and Nekrich's 1986 history of the USSR, with the phrase "sexual utopianism," which I remembered from a talk by columnist Joe Sobran. I could think of no appropriate venue for the essay, but having previously contributed to *The Occidental Quarterly*, I offered first refusal to that journal. I owe editor Kevin Lamb a debt of gratitude for taking a chance on a provocative piece which I had no professional qualifications for writing.

Over the next three years I expanded on my ideas in the following five pieces included in this collection, three of which take the modest form of review essays. The final essay was written recently.

These pieces are only a small fraction of what I have published over the years, but have received more attention than all the rest put together. Clearly, the issues I discuss strike a chord in many readers. Most interesting to me was the generational pattern in responses I got. Older men who dated and got married in the 1960s or before were more likely to condemn my viewpoint and assume I must be a bitter misogynist. But the same essays attracted a cult-like following among mostly younger men on the internet. Some of these young men have approached me to thank me for explaining for them the mysterious and irrational female behavior they have seen all their lives but had never before understood.

One response I received is so remarkable that I must quote it. Several times over the course of these essays I have referred to Thomas Fleming as a good representative of Christian traditionalism. I once made a half-hearted attempt politely to introduce some of my ideas on a *Chronicles* website discussion thread, suggesting that he and similar writers might profit from studying unconstrained female sexuality directly (as opposed to theological pronouncements on sexual morality or historical family law). I was told that I was a "misogynist" due my personal "difficulties with women," that I was guilty of "demean[ing] the character of women" and "indulg[ing] in fantasies about female sexuality" and that the "this is not the place to air [my] grievances." Farther along he added:

> I know too well how many Men's Movement androgynes are looking for a reason to get back at the women who have ruined their lives. I am warning them from the outset that there is no place in this discussion for their battered egos, wounded vanities, and whining exaltations of a male supremacy

. . . etc., etc. Fleming is acknowledged even by his admirers to be a bit of a nut, but his bizarre *ad hominem* overreaction mirrors the weaknesses of too many traditional conservatives.

On the internet, I have come across stories of men kicked out of their churches for discussing the sorts of ideas contained in my essays. Weblogs like Dalrock and Patriactionary have done a good job of cataloguing the cluelessness of Christian pastors and even their collusion in perverting traditional teachings in order to make them more palatable to the *Cosmo*-girls in their pews.

But among the younger generation, something is changing.

Ideas like those exposed here are reaching wide readerships. I did not have a lot of company when I began the intellectual journey which produced these essays. Now I am merely one voice among many. An entire so-called manosphere—*androsphere* might have been a better label—has grown up on the internet in response to feminism and the actual behavior of contemporary women. Even the enemy has begun to take notice. The feminist-traditionalist consensus that men are primarily responsible for women's problems and poor relations between the sexes has been challenged, and there is no going back.

Finally, I wish to note that I do not consider myself a "men's rights activist." This label, which I have more than once seen applied to myself, reflects a moral sensibility common in our age, but one which I do not share. Men should not be encouraged to see themselves as yet another of many competing aggrieved identity groups. If I must be labeled, a better choice of words might be "women's duties activist." I also agree heartily with Stephen Baskerville's view that what are called "men's rights" in our current debased political vernacular are really men's duties: our duty to display moral leadership for the long term benefit of our descendants, both women and men.

INDEX

ABOUT THE AUTHOR

F. ROGER DEVLIN, Ph.D. is an independent scholar. He is the author of *Alexandre Kojève and the Outcome of Modern Thought* (Lanham, M.D.: University Press of America, 2004) and many essays and reviews in such publications as *The Occidental Quarterly*, *American Renaissance*, Counter-Currents/*North American New Right*, *VDare*, *Modern Age*, *The Social Contract*, *Alternative Right*, and *The Last Ditch*. A bibliography of his work is available online at http://devliniana.wordpress.com/.

www.ingramcontent.com/pod-product-compliance
Lightning Source LLC
Chambersburg PA
CBHW031432270326
41930CB00007B/675